ALPHABET OF FAITH

ALPHABET OF FAITH

PROPHETIC PRAYERS FOR A CHAOTIC WORLD

WALTER BRUEGGEMANN

CONRAD L. KANAGY
EDITOR

FORTRESS PRESS
Minneapolis

ALPHABET OF FAITH
Prophetic Prayers for a Chaotic World

30 29 28 27 26 25 2 3 4 5 6 7 8 9

Library of Congress Cataloging-in-Publication Data

Names: Brueggemann, Walter, author. | Kanagy, Conrad L., editor.
Title: Alphabet of faith : prophetic prayers for a chaotic world / Walter Brueggemann ; Conrad L. Kanagy, editor.
Description: Minneapolis : Fortress Press, [2025]
Identifiers: LCCN 2024055037 (print) | LCCN 2024055038 (ebook) | ISBN 9798889834731 (hardback) | ISBN 9798889834748 (ebook)
Subjects: LCSH: Prayers.
Classification: LCC BV245 .B677 2025 (print) | LCC BV245 (ebook) | DDC 242/.8--dc23/eng/20250108
LC record available at https://lccn.loc.gov/2024055037
LC ebook record available at https://lccn.loc.gov/2024055038

Cover image: Stock images from iStock
Cover design: Laurie Ingram Art + Design.com

Print ISBN: 979-8-8898-3473-1
eBook ISBN: 979-8-8898-3474-8

CONTENTS

PREFACE

There is no good rhyme or reason to line out matters according to the alphabet. This is so even though many before me have also done so. I suggest that the primary gain of such an alphabetic listing is heuristic. That is, the sequence of letters invites one to think what might be a next item on the list. And after the list is completed, one might consider what alternatives could have been chosen in place of the present listing. Thus with my present list, you, as a reader, along with me are also invited to consider what alternatives might have been included. One might begin by considering the letter *Q* for which there are not so many options. I have entered a rather anachronistic usage of **quick** that functions here as a noun meaning "the living," as in "the quick and the dead." There are of course some alternatives, even for *Q*.

It will be evident that the list I offer is a bit random, as there are items I have particularly wanted to accent. In addition to *quick*, my topics may be readily organized into four unequal groups: faith, critical thinking, church tradition, and people.

The first and largest group of entries concerns dimensions of the substance and practice of biblical faith. I note the following items in this group of entries.

First, there is the entry of **YHWH**, the God of Israel whose name is unpronounceable in its hiddenness; **holiness** is the quite distinctive marker of YHWH's singularity, a modifier that precedes even our favorite affirmation that God is love. Before all else, YHWH is holy in awesome unapproachability.

Under the general rubric of **faith**, we may also include:

- the practice of **covenant**
- the discipline of **prayer**
- the gift of **emancipation** and expectation of **victory**
- **knowledge of God** that is given as God's self-revelation
- he practice of **lament** and confidence in God's victory over **death**
- the study of **scrolls** and appreciation of scroll-power

Second, under critical thinking whereby we may reflect on social power I have included the following:

- **academia**, a mixed blessing concerning both human knowledge and the force of ideology
- **nationalism**, a readiness to absolutize a particular arrangement of power according to one's self-interest
- **totalism**, a readiness to substitute a particular claim as though it were the whole
- **xenophobia**, a fearfulness of the other

Each of these entries concerns the way in which our best reasoning can serve us well or can be distorted by ideology or self-illusion.

Third I have included two markers of my own church tradition because they are now so urgently required in our current climate of eager ideological combat:

- **irenic**, a practice and posture that seeks peaceable harmony in the church without undue preoccupation with theological precision
- **union**, an old passion in my church tradition reaching back to the Prussian Union in Germany wherein Christians of various confessions could be together in worship and mission, even in their differences

Fourth, I have included eight names of specific people. Four of these concern contemporary scholars who have greatly impacted me for good:

- Karl **Barth** is for me, as for many, an immense challenge but also an immense resource for thinking and practicing faith in our postmodern context.
- Gerhard **von Rad** has been my lodestar in Old Testament study; when I first learned of his work via Davie Napier, I was smitten and continue to be smitten by his capacity for "magic" with the text.
- Norman **Gottwald** is second to me in Old Testament study because he introduced me, as he did so many others, to a social scientific study of the text with reference to economics.
- D. W. **Winnicott**, childhood psychiatrist, has been central not only for my understanding of the dialogic nature

of human personhood but also for me in arriving at some form of health and integration.

The other four names included are characters in the biblical narrative. They include **Moses**, the founder, **Jeremiah**, the great prophet of the exile, and **Zechariah**, the father of John the Baptizer, who broke his silence at the birth of his son. The odd man out in this quartet is **Omri**, the founder of the strongest and longest running dynasty of the Northern Kingdom of Israel. He can be a stand-in for all of those who exhibit great power in public, but who score low, if at all, on the Deuteronomic calculus of covenantal fidelity.

It is my hope that this set of brief expositions will be suggestive for the reader, so that the reader may do the work of constructing similar "alphabets" of our most treasured and our most problematic legacy. As is always the case now, I am indebted to Conrad Kanagy for suggesting this project and seeing it through to publication.

—Walter Brueggemann, October 2024

EDITOR'S INTRODUCTION

WALTER BRUEGGEMANN WAS born the son of a preacher. But not just any preacher—a preacher with a soft demeanor in an age where not all preachers were known for their gentleness, kindness, and compassion. And he was born the son of a "union man," humble, uneducated, but formed from the soil of the Prussian Union that sought to end theological quarrels in the New Rhineland of the Missouri River Valley. To love God and neighbor. To extend a high level of tolerance to theological difference. To express an irenic Christian faith where "in all things charity" ruled the day. August, the dad to whom Walter was born and who turned out to be his pastor, and the religious culture that formed that pastor, made all the difference in the man, and the healing ministry to pastors that Walter ultimately became. August is a constant reference point for Walter across his ninety years—a touchstone as it were.

But first Walter would have to deal with Edwin, the second of the Brueggemann sons. August and Hilda Brueggemann gave birth to Walter on March 13, 1933, the last of three sons. The oldest, Charles, died as an infant. Edwin as the second played the role of eldest brother and played it well. Photos of the two boys consistently show Ed out front and Walter behind. Ed was loud and brusque and a bit of a showoff.

Walter was exceedingly shy, slow to speak, and certainly slow to show off. Ed never quite lived up to his bravado and Walter quietly but surely overachieved in everything even while feeling as though he was behind Ed and everyone else.

This "Walter come lately" attitude was building in Walter, if not resentment, then surely a fierce determination to prove himself, if not the better of the two remaining brothers, the better of just about everyone else. Without knowing it perhaps, Walter was grinding an axe that he would use most of his life as he built a reputation in the 1980s to the 2020s as the most prolific Old Testament scholar of his generation, if not of all time. While he would often repeat that "every text or biblical author has an axe to grind, and that good exegesis required discovering what exactly that axe was," so Brueggemann would continue swinging at his own body of work, pommeling it, as St. Paul says, into submission.

Still, it would take a while for Walter to get over his "Harvey Cox" days when he dreamed of making the kind of waves in the religious and popular world that Cox did. He finally made peace with his calling to the church and to pastors and would-be pastors. Being the son of "Pop" Brueggemann, as young pastors would come to call August, was probably key to finding this peace. Thirty of these pastors showed up at "Pop's" funeral to sing in one harmonious voice the anthem of the Prussian Union:

Now thank we all our God
with heart and hands and voices,
who wondrous things has done,
in whom his world rejoices;

who from our mothers' arms
has blessed us on our way
with countless gifts of love,
and still is ours today.

O may this bounteous God
through all our life be near us,
with ever joyful hearts
and blessed peace to cheer us,
to keep us in his grace,
and guide us when perplexed,
and free us from all ills
of this world in the next.

For while Walter found his mother Hilda overly protective, overly demanding, and overly anxious—always worried that Ed or Walter or August would eventually bring shame on the family through some errant mishap, August became the one to whom Brueggemann attached and would aspire to emulate. In fact, it is quite likely that Brueggemann's lifelong and extraordinary commitment to the training, healing, nurturing, and calling of pastors to faithful prophetic witness came most from his relationship to his father. "My dad would be very proud of me. He used to write little notes of encouragement to me on half pieces of paper. I often wondered what happened to the other half." Walter's healing touch with pastors came from his ongoing desire to bring healing to his father's wounds, suffered as abuse at the hands of strict church boards and perhaps what he perceived as his strict and rigid, although well-intended, wife who carried her own loss and trauma.

Hilda Brueggemann was an anxious and moralistic creature who lived in fear that she would lose her boys and that they might cause her to lose everything else. This was a troubling relationship for Walter as would be the marriage that followed and that reflected elements of his childhood constraints. He yearned for freedom, and as he began to experience it spiritually and theologically, he would also experience it in his relationships, both intimate and otherwise. "I wrote to be free. To be in that unconstrained place of emancipation."

Walter's attachment to his father won the day when it came to his relationship with God. Those who knew him in an earlier time of his life, often remark on the substantial change in his demeanor and affect as he grew older and the increased warmth and affection that he expressed to those around him. When it came time for a vocational decision to be made, the decision was easy. Walter would simply follow his father, as he recounts in this conversation from 2022:

> Well, I thought, when I decided, I was pre-theological was what we called it, I assumed I would go through college and seminary. And do what my dad did. I thought I could do that and I had great admiration for what he did, and my horizon was fairly small. I didn't understand much about the great issues. But I could see that the way he was spending his life was really important and that's what I wanted to do. So, it was the personal admiration for Dad

> as I knew him, but also the admiration for the ministry that he had that I remember. In 1945, when the war ended, like every church we had stars up front for all the people in service. And we had one gold star for one death, and I remember the special liturgy we had of taking those stars down and returning them to the families. I remember my dad presiding over that with his great passion for grace. That was a very defining kind of moment I saw in his work as a pastor.

And so it was that both Walter and Edward would be ordained as a second generation of union men in St. Paul's Evangelical and Reformed congregation in Blackburn, Missouri, the place of Walter's greatest childhood formation. There is no doubt that Walter's relationship with his father impacted how he saw father-and-son relationships in the Scripture, how he understood the relationship between the divine Father and Son, and how he came to mentor so many sons and daughters of the church. Given the value that his father placed on education, it is not surprising that Walter's first prayer in this collection is entitled "*A* is for Academia."

His second prayer is entitled "*B* is for Barth," that is, Karl Barth. Perhaps no other theologian had greater influence on Brueggemann. But this influence was sharpened by his relationship with another Barthian scholar—Brevard Childs of Yale University. One of Childs's former students quibbled with my description in Walter's biography of the longtime tension between him and Childs: "But surely you have exaggerated the tension in the relationship between Walter and Brevard. Walter once told me that he deeply appreciated

Brevard—that they even took in a professional baseball game together." This response is reflective of the complex relationship between these two twentieth-century giants of biblical scholarship. It is also illustrative of Walter's ability to express respect with criticism of a peer in the field.

In fact, Brueggemann is quoted in Childs's 2007 obituary published by Yale University: "With almost no conversation partners in the 20th century whom he regards as consistently reliable or worthy of consideration (with the decisive exception of Barth), Childs has staked out a position and vocation for biblical theology that is sure to reshape our common work and that will require intense engagement by any who dare take up the task."

While the complexity was perhaps nuanced in part by Walter's ongoing insecurity about his position in biblical scholarship relative to Ivy League divinity schools, it is also most keenly related to the view that each held of the biblical text that both loved so dearly and that both were committed to interpreting faithfully. And to their differing views of Karl Barth—but more on that in a moment. Born within months of each other in 1923, Childs was a son of the South born in Colombia, South Carolina, who, though trained in the North, would retain views of Scripture that Brueggemann found restrictive, rigid, and "Sunday Schoolish." Walter grew up on the wide-open plains of the Midwest and openness to the way one reads, interprets, and lives out the biblical text continued to evolve and be a key ingredient of his life and work. Brueggemann took risks with attacks and with the God of the text that Brevard would never have dreamed of doing. Childs's work was largely technical, monographic, and for the scholarly guild. Walter's writing was always for the church, not the "wise and learned of the church," but for those like his father August who came out of obedience and faithfulness to the ministry calling. They came with few tools to guide their preaching or their pastorate. Walter's goal was always to add value to their toolbox.

Walter was trained as a sociologist as an undergraduate at Elmhurst College. By the late 1960s he was already including sociologist Peter Berger as required reading in his courses. Berger, among other interpretive scholars, helped Walter to understand that the biblical text must be interpreted as an open book: socially constructed within context and that must be interpreted within context.

While not a theologian, Berger expresses his own distaste for the explanations of Sunday school. "If you prefer the explanations you received in Sunday school, you will not find poison of a sociological approach particularly appealing," to paraphrase Berger. And what is this poison? It is the ongoing understanding that the reality that we see in front of us now is not all that exists. There are alternative realities that must be constantly interrogated and investigated.

And this perhaps is the greatest rub between Brueggemann and some of his peers like Childs. Walter saw the world beyond what was, beyond what is, and even beyond what will be. The prophetic imagination would be Brueggemann's defining thesis and is described by him as the "capacity to see and host an alternative world to the one that lies in front of us." But believing in that alternative world and then having the courage to speak that world into being, is risky business, says Brueggemann. "Few have the courage to take these risks," Brueggemann once told me.

The major theological difference between Childs and Brueggemann is related to how they each interpreted Karl Barth, father of the German Confessing Church. Barth was a Swiss Reformed theologian and likely accounts for Walter's embrace of the sovereignty of God and his commitment to the open-endedness of the biblical text and the God of that text. And the two are connected.

Walter's colleague Kathleen O'Connor argues that the sovereignty of God is the "deepest sense" of Brueggemann's, and that it is more than intellectual. It is also deeply personal: "In theological terms the sovereignty of God is the sense that God is the ruler of and decider. God is the one, and even if you don't have a literal understanding that every little thing is because God wants it to happen. Even if you have a wide-open sense of reality—in the middle of that is the sovereign God. And that came from Barth."

Brueggemann himself says of Barth: "Had he lived longer he would have written more volumes [of *Church Dogmatics*, which was incomplete when Barth died] because it's all open ended and is being unfolded further and further by the power of the Gospel." Barth's big phrase was "God is wholly and completely different from us, and there is no point of contact, except for God's reach to us in grace." He wanted to combat all natural theology that he thought led straight to Adolf Hitler's idea that the German people were God's chosen folk and that God was dwelling among them. Late in life, Barth wanted to say, "No! God has nothing to do with any of that!" So, Barth needs very much to be understood in the context of a Nazi crisis.

In a 2001 letter to Carey Newman, then editor at Westminster John Knox Press, Brueggemann perhaps differentiates himself from Childs best:

> I am aware always of the huge commonality that Childs and I have, but I want to make two caveats about that. First, I am endlessly discomforted by his readiness to label me and call names and dismiss me. First, a "Neo-Marxist" and then a "Gnostic." I simply think that such labels do not help us at all. Second, I believe that he is reductionistic in moving from the language to the reality . . . I do not doubt that there is reality behind the language, but I believe that our proper study in doing biblical theology is to study what the language says. . . . I do not think it is the business of biblical scholars to launch into extravagant ontological and confessional claims [e.g. Sunday School categories]. To be sure, I do some of that, but I am not militant or preemptive about it in the way that he is.

One of the greatest pet peeves of Walter Brueggemann is to be reduced or categorized or typified. Just like he resists doing that to the biblical text, or the God of that text.

And he was not at all against Sunday school by the way. As early as 1965, he had published a little essay for Sunday School teachers in a church periodical (*Church School Worker*), describing the most effective way to write or study or teach the story or biography of biblical characters:

1. Study the historical context to determine the particular crisis of faith.
2. Consider the theological issue as it relates to God.
3. Consider how God intervenes in the event to deal with the crisis.
4. Determine how the person involved is a participant in the purposes of God.

In Brueggemann's theology, God is always the primary actor. And that God is a free God. And the activity of humanity is always done—both in the biblical text and today—within the context of this God who is at once emancipated and sovereign and who desires that all of creation be free as well. Though both were highly influenced by Luther and the Lutheran tradition, the effect of Calvin on Brueggemann's reading of the biblical text and the God of that text is unmistakable in the differences between these two—Childs and Brueggemann. And the difference in interpreting Barth between the two accounted for more differences than either may have realized. This difference is seen quite dramatically in Brueggemann's appeal for the church to embrace LGBGT+ individuals in the church. It is difficult to imagine that Childs's reading of Barth would lead him to the same place as Brueggemann.

The third prayer entitled "*C* is for Covenant" emerges out of Walter's view of God's sovereignty, and the sovereignty embedded in God's covenant with humankind. In 2020, at the outset of Covid-19, I began a blog and podcast called *The Church Dismantled*. My thesis was that because of the church's failure at God's mission, God was undoing the socially constructed church of the twenty-first century in order to reveal what was core to the church. That is, Jesus Christ and the mission of God to care for the world that God "so loved" and as I said, "so loves still." I did not imagine this to be a particularly controversial idea. I rather assumed that anyone with their eyes half open and who knew something about the American church would get the idea. For the church was in a freefall. Rapidly aging. Youth running away as quickly as they could. Young families opting for baseball or some other event rather than church services. Childbirth rates declining. A church that has hunkered down and cozied up to Donald Trump and the MAGA movement. A church that denies it's racist origins and ongoing reinforcement of white supremacy. And on and on.

I thought it was as simple as pointing out that God had done the same thing to God's people in 587 BCE. In my simplicity however, I forgot how God's people received the prophetic word of exile then. Because as it turns out, Jeremiah faced opposition time and again until the unforeseeable became foreseeable, and Nebuchadnezzar hauled God's people off to their worst nightmare: an extended vacation with their enemies to the north. And as usual, God soon caught up with Jeremiah who then caught up with God's people and gave them the most unbelievable news yet. This was not exile, this was not a vacation, and this was not a punishment. This was a mission project. A missional moment for the people of God. A season in which they were promised Shalom only if they brought Shalom to the people of Babylon.

And while I was not thrown into a pit for my thesis that the church is dismantling, I did find myself facing quite a bit of opposition, especially from the hometown crowd. I soon resigned from the ministry.

In hopes of finding out whether I was as crazy as some people thought, I reached out to Walter Brueggemann who has, more than anyone else, worked with the book of Jeremiah and the exile of God's people to Babylon. Not only did Walter embrace the idea he added a twist related to the crucifixion that I had never considered.

> If you think systemically then you can see the crucifixion and the resurrection of Jesus as a dismantling, and a rebuilding. And when those categories are assigned only to the person of Jesus, as evangelicals do, then you do not understand that the same narrative of crucifixion and resurrection is the narrative of the church.

I came to understand that one of the most threatening parts of what Brueggemann brought to his work was his commitment to understanding that God was sovereign. Brueggemann had a long-standing debate with another Old Testament theologian, Terry Fretheim of Luther Seminary, about this idea, and Brueggemann never budged. Fretheim argued that God's faithfulness was expressed through the hands and feet of God's people. And he was scathing in his critique of Brueggemann. But Brueggemann had no time for placing God in the hands of human beings and their work in the world—he had seen what a mess we can make of that world.

While visiting Walter some time ago, I mentioned the ongoing tension with Fretheim over the sovereign nature of God. He chuckled and said, "I think that sovereignty is what it means to be God." Brueggemann argued, against the positions of other theologians deeply influenced by the Enlightenment (as we all are), particularly the vast majority who embraced historical criticism, that God could intervene in the world whenever God wanted. Even if doing so reflected a change in what God had promised previously. Walter chafes at the restrictions we have placed on God and a theology that restricts God's movement. At the heart of Brueggemann's theology is the belief that God is free and emancipated.

But the reaction of some reminded me of what a difficult "sell" this argument of God's sovereignty remains in the dimming shadows of modernity. Sociologist Max Weber, a century ago, anticipated the aversion of modern folks to just about anything we would be unable to understand, control, count, or predict. This is to say, he latently predicted our aversion to a sovereign God who we cannot fully understand, predict, or control. The Enlightenment diminished divinity and elevated humanity. It weakened mystery and strengthened certainty.

Thus, Weber argued that the rationalization of society emerging from the Enlightenment would diminish the capacity of modern people to be creative, accept mystery, and live with anything beyond our empirical abilities. He predicted that the "iron cage of rationality" would entrap modern individuals within a world where control, prediction, efficiency, and counting would be the highest good. In such a world that we have all absorbed subconsciously through our culture, it is no surprise that progressives have gotten rid of

God and the Bible, and conservatives have created a God who is predictable, controllable, and captive to their particular categories of sin and righteousness. Dear God! The Sovereign has little room to squirm or to be God!

But what if, as Brueggemann suggests, being God is to be anything but efficient, predictable, controllable, and quantifiable? What if God is outside the bounds of most of what we have socially constructed and called real, including the church? Why would God not dismantle such a thing made within the confines and image of modernity—with its endless committees, bylaws, constitutions, councils, and so on? Not to mention denominational structures, which are primarily about paying staff salaries, finding new language to do the same old things, and rearranging the furniture on a ship ever diminishing in size. Brueggemann once mused to me that only the mediocre desire to lead denominations these days, for who else would wish to captain a sinking ship!

The resistance by folks to my blog and podcast should not have surprised me. They assumed that by saying God is sovereign, God controls and wills everything that happens. I believe neither. But I still believe that God is sovereign over that which God may not control and over that which God does not will.

The difficulty of accepting a sovereign God reflects our weak-kneed spirituality that resists submitting to anything except our own sovereignty. We left Great Britain to be free of the monarchy's sovereignty only to put in motion a nation built on the individual's freedom. It's becoming clear where that is taking us as a church and nation.

But this I know from reading the saints for thirty years. Submission was their central value. That is what made them saints, just as sovereignty makes God who God is. We can submit to the Sovereign or try to be the sovereign. But if we choose the latter, the tower will always come tumbling down.

The Psalmist's words hauntingly remind us that when "The kings of the earth set themselves, and the rulers take counsel together against the Lord," there is a lot of derisive laughter in the heavens. The church is not immune from setting itself against the Lord, and when it does so, why would the Lord not dismantle the church? And even chuckle while doing so?

And so it is that Walter's view of God as sovereign, but bound by a free covenant with humankind, is the back story to this third prayer. Each of the remaining prayers in this volume emerge from some historic relationship of Brueggemann with God and others who deeply influenced him. In this way these twenty-six prayers represent the most unique presentation of his prayers to date. They are autobiographical, theological, and sociological. They are, as close as we can get, to the exegetical method of the biblical text by Walter Brueggemann.

A is for Academia

You, holy God,
    have commanded us to love you
        with our minds as well as with our
        heart, soul, and might.
We thank you for the capacity to think
    boldly and honestly in your presence,
        that we need not fear serious thought,
        that we need not shrink from critical thinking,
        that we need not cower before honesty.
We are grateful for the long tradition of teachers who have blessed us with thought,
    for rabbis and sages,
    for professors and instructors,
    for tutors and teachers in every age
        who have sought to serve you and obey you with their minds.
We are mindful of our ready seduction to false thinking,
    for the force of ideology in our lives,
    for the seduction of self-interest that clouds our clarity.

We are aware of the way in which
our busy minds can be factories for idols,
that talk us out of the truth of your governance.
We pray your good blessing on our
schools, academies, and universities,
that they may be citadels of truth-telling,
and not agencies of foolishness.
Given our best thinking
and our most discerning learning,
we do confess that
knowing you and obeying you is the beginning of all our wisdom,
and the conclusion of all our wonderment.
We would be like the ancient magi
who arrived at you by following their best learning.
Like them, we would bring you our best gifts;
like them, we would bow down in awe before you; and
like them, we would return home in a different way,
gladly chastened, instructed, and empowered,
for a new and different life
lived in response to your good purpose.
We pray in the name of Jesus who confounded the learned in the temple. Amen.

B is for Barth

We give you hearty thanks for your good and faithful witness, Karl
who early in his life saw that you are fully unlike any of your creatures,
who saw later in his life that you bear the marks of fragility and vulnerability
common to our human lot.
We give thanks for his great energy,
that produced more pages than we can digest,
or perhaps than we can even read.
We give you thanks for his bravery,
as he stood, sometimes quite alone,
against the evil of fascism all around him.
We give you thanks for his courage,
wherein he told the truth about our needful world,
wherein he led the church into what boldness it could muster.
We give you thanks for his innocence
wherein he trusted in your gospel
enough to settle for, "Yes, Jesus loves me."

He lived by your good grace as he knew he must:
he was slow to accept Roman Catholics as a proper part of your faithful church;
he was even slower to accept Judaism as a serious form of faith;
he lived a compromised, complex life with the triangle in his home.
It is not for us to judge his life,
but rather to learn from it;
for we too are slow to accept Christians other than our own kind;
for we too are slow to recognizes the legitimacy of the other;
for we too live compromised lives, so that we too live your good grace.
We are full of wonder and appreciation
for the ways in which he himself kept growing in his faith;
for the ways in which he refused to offer a closed system of his faith,
for the ways in which he loved you with his whole mind,
along with his heart, his soul, and his might;
for his puckish humor that prevented him from too much self-seriousness.
Teach us to treasure his work,
to be instructed and empowered by his witness,

to trust, as he did, the leading of your Spirit into fresh directions that keep us off-balance.
We finish grateful for the vitality of his faith
that continues to gift us in generative ways
with fresh insight, and
new courage, and
resistant hope,
in full confidence in your good governance.
We pray in the name of Jesus whom he embraced fully as the truth of our lives
and of his life. Amen.

C IS FOR COVENANT

We are left in awe and wonder
 at the splendor of your holiness.
All the more, we are dazzled and stunned
 by your willingness for covenantal interaction,
 a holy God risking the loyalty of relatedness.
We are thankful for your post-flood covenant
 with "every living creature of all flesh."
 Thus we may imagine you in loyal love
 with radishes and rabbits,
 with whales and weeds,
 with maize and muskrats,
 all held in your presence.
We give thanks for your singular unilateral reach toward
 Father Abraham, Mother Sarah and their long-running family,
 whereby you performed powerful blessings
 through you chosen for us all.

We give thanks for your smoke-enveloped presence
with Moses at Sinai in your bilateral readiness,
for your Ten urgent requirements,
for your long lingering promises of well-being toward the faithful,
for your impatience with our idolatries, and
for your reception of our grateful offerings.
We are grateful for the uncommon wisdom and courage
of old King Josiah
who called your chosen ones back to covenant
after royal centuries of idolatry,
as we learn through him that you are indeed the
God of second, and third, and fourth chances,
for your readiness to re-embrace your wayward people when it is too late for them.
We are grateful for the staggering hope of Jeremiah,
who anticipated your new covenant that you would offer,
a newness for your long-running chosen people,
a newness concerning a new people of chosenness.
comprising the multitudes too long rejected as "no people."
We affirm that your "new covenant" sets off possibilities for
renewal, restoration, and response.

We are grateful for the new meal of bread and wine,
or as we say,
the supper of "his body and blood,"
"broken and poured out,"
whereby we drink "the cup of the new covenant,"
and receive a forgiven life back from you.
On all these counts, for your generous self-giving
for the sake of our new life and the life of the world,
we give you thanks
as we ponder how your holiness is willingly given away for our sake.
And now in our gratitude
we pledge ourselves to covenant
with you that we will shun our compelling idols
of nation, race, and gender
to love only you with our hearts and minds,
to love our neighbors—
especially the ones in need,
that we may be life-giving
to share the life you give us,
that we may be repairers of the breach,
stepping into the broken places among us
with healing resolve,

that we may be reconcilers to overcome the fearful divides among us.

God of all our covenant-making,

be alongside us in our reach for covenanting,

that your whole creation may be newly knit together in loyal love,

filled with wonder, love, and praise. Amen.

D IS FOR DEATH

We count our days;
 when younger we imagine our days to be countless;
 then, caught up short,
  by illness,
  by injury,
  by abandonment,
  by catastrophe;
 we sense how contingent we are,
  like the flower that fades,
  like the grass that withers.
Some of us are blessed into old age,
 with our death as a "natural passing"
  that we may sleep with our fathers and mothers.
Some of us not so blessed,
 finding death to be a threat beyond our management.
 It may be then that we call death by its old mythic name, *Mot*,
  the God of death,
  the threat to life,

the disturber of the created order,
the enemy of our future,
the contrary adversary of the holy God.
When we utter the name, we may sense our helplessness,
that we cry out in resignation,
aware of the surging power of Mot
with his plagues, and
with his destructiveness,
that blinds us to your compassion.
We are summoned by our faith to be stone-cold sober about death,
not to deny it,
not to make it sweet,
not to pretend it away with cosmetic covering,
but to know and acknowledge that death lingers as a threat:
it lingers for much of the world in poverty and famine;
it lingers in too many places through war and violence;
it lingers among us in medical diagnoses,
enough to evoke despair,
to cause us to cry out in lament,
to weep at endings come too soon,
to curse you when we must for your neglectful silence,
with our abandonment to the powers of darkness.
We are left with mighty lament;
we are summoned to bitter complaint;

we are coerced into honest doubt.
And then . . . sometimes . . .
not always but sometimes . . .
our lament turns to praise,
our complaint morphs into affirmation, and
our doubt spooks to singing hope.
We transpose early acknowledgements of the power of Mot
into mocking:
O Mot—where is your victory!
Mot has no victory but is defeated by you, the God of life!
O Mot—where is your sting?
Mot has lost his stinger,
overwhelmed by the antidote of your goodness!

We do not believe innocently,
or easily,
or on the cheap,
but sometimes we trust in your assurance
that you prevail as the God of life.
We stand alongside the women at the empty tomb;
we sit at the table with the astonished disciples,
we have new prospects as we confess
That Christ is risen, risen indeed,

that death is conquered,
that Mot is defeated.
We tell the old story of our risen power;
what we cannot tell, we sing;
we sing to you in gladness;
we sing out loud in defiance;
we sing together in deep affirmation;
we sing without embarrassment
that you are the Lord of life,
that you override the cosmic negations we see so clearly,
that your capacity for newness surges among us in ways we do not understand.
We may term it "Easter";
or resurrection,
or new creation,
many names for the inexplicable openness you make possible in the world
as our worlds are shattered by our powerful, hidden purpose.
Right in the midst of our despair,
You make all things new
often enough that we trust you,
as we praise you,
and we wait for your good governance. Amen.

E IS FOR EMANCIPATION

Pharaoh occupies front and center

in the exploitation of workers,

and in the reduction of peasants to slaves.

Pharaoh, ever at the center of the universe

with all power and wealth . . .

until you answered the cry of the slaves.

Once you answered their cry,

you joined issue with Pharaoh;

you issued your lordly command for freedom:

"Let my people go!"

You sent the mighty waters.

By the end of the story Miriam was empowered to sing,

as we sing with her:

Sing to YHWH;

sing to YHWH who drowned Pharaoh's horses and all other emblems of ruthless power;

sing to YHWH who has destroyed Pharaoh's chariots and all other vehicles of control.

So we sing;
So we sing to you, the great emancipator;
So we sing all the way to Sinai,
    where we have embraced your covenant of freedom,
    and the Ten Requirements for neighborly freedom.
But Pharaoh persists, even in the face of your freedom.
    He takes many names variously,
        Tiglath-Pileser, Sennacherib, Nebuchadnezzar . . . all the way to Caesar.
    All these several Pharaohs have in mind the same
        monopolies of grain, wealth, power, and slaves.

We have ringing in our ears your mandate:
    Let my people go!
    Let the widows, orphans, and immigrants go from coercive exploitation;
    Let the publicans and sinners go from their social exclusion;
    Let the blind and the deaf and the lepers go from their disability;
    Let the poor go from their helpless indebtedness.
We sing the old freedom song of Miriam,
        and we witness Jesus, the emancipator,
    as he let his people go free from fear and exploitation,
    as he confronted the demanding power of Rome,

as he confounded the Roman governor with the question of truth.

In the end we know that we are unfree not only because of doubt and fear,

but because of "Satan, sin, death,"

that is, the demonic force of ideology.

You—in your splendor—

have confronted all of the falsities with your truth telling;

you stood before the Roman governor,

and before the Jewish council,

and before he imperial centurion,

you in your innocence,

you in your truthfulness.

Eventually you declared the law of Rome to be null and void;

You reckoned "the law" as obsolete.

You dispatched among us the great apostle of freedom:

"for freedom you have set free."

And then you have dispatched a series of ambassadors of your freedom.

We are glad to name Martin Luther who set us free for your grace,

Charles Darwin who set us free from old static reality;

Karl Marx who set us free from economic illusion and mystification;

Sigmund Freud who set us free from imprisoned selves.

And in our time another Martin and his galaxy of companions
who would not turn back,
who have broken the bondage of racism.
The force of Pharaoh persists even now among us,
with wealth mal-distributed;
with power narrowly monopolized;
with truth devolving into ideology;
with scientism that knows too much,
and technology that easily talks us out of our humanness.
It is for good reason that we turn to you,
the one who frees us from sexism
"neither male nor female,"
the one who frees us from fearful sectarianism,
"neither Jew nor Greek,"
the one who frees us from rabid nationalism,
as the Lord of all nations.
We pray now for goodly portions of your emancipatory Spirit,
that we may be relentlessly on the side of freedom,
resistant to enslaving ideology of any ilk,
opposed to the exploitative economics, unjust politics, and
hood-winking religion.
That we might sing, "Free at last"
and long before.

We pray in the emancipatory name of Jesus
    who stilled the waters,
    who cast out the demons,
    who fed the hungry . . .
        all acts of your genuine freedom. Amen.

F IS FOR FAITH

Now faith is the assurance of things hoped for,
the conviction of things not seen (Hebrews 11:1).
What a mouthful!
It is our declaration that we do not live by what we see,
nor by what is in front of us.
We live, rather,
by what you have said,
by what you have promised,
by what you intend.
You have promised a creation that is well-ordered and abundant,
with sufficient provision for all creatures,
the birds, the fish, the creeping things.
You have promised a society of justice
in which the vulnerable are protected,
in which the poor have adequate provision,
in which wealth serves the entire community.
You have promised families, clans, and tribes of faithful love,
of respect for all parties,
of dignity and security for every member.

You have uttered such a mouthful!
We take your sweeping promises as resolve for a different world,
one glimpsed in the Exodus emancipation and the Sinai covenant,
one identified in the reform of Ezra and the founding of Judaism,
one we know in the emancipatory ministry of Jesus
that culminates in his Easter power for life.
We are gladly on the receiving end of your wondrous promises.

We do not doubt your promises,
nor your resolve to keep them.
We do not worry about your power to fulfill them,
or your steadfastness in keeping them.
For that reason,
we respond to your vision of a good creation
by our generous management of your creation,
by taking good care to protect streams and forests,
cherishing every wild animal and every odd species of plant.
we respond to your promise of a just society
by the generosity of neighborly love,
by the passage of laws that regulate wealth,

by policies that protect the dignity of every person,
by attentiveness to the weak,
the disabled, and the vulnerable.
We respond to your promise of communities of love,
by our glad participation in such communities
that looks beyond self-interest,
that practices hospitality toward the unwelcome,
that performs forgiveness for affront and injury, and
that exhibits generosity in self-giving practices.
We are glad to stand
in the company of the great performers of faith,
as their names easily roll off our lips:
by faith Abraham . . .
by faith Jacob . . .
by faith Moses . . .
and then a whole procession of the faithful:
by faith Martin with his dreams,
by faith Walter with his auto workers,
by faith Eleanor with her UN votes,
by faith Norman with his relentless socialism,
by faith Jim as leader in the company of sojourners,
by faith Desmond with his joy in justice,
by faith Shane with his habitat at the edge,

by faith Angela with her passion for viable world order,
and by faith all the company of those
who refuse to let our unjust world go unchallenged,
who run risks and dare disruption for the sake of the neighbor,
who live lives of unseemly joy amid a world of violation.
We must, in response to your promises, confess
that we have sought to reduce your promises to syllogisms,
that we have tried to transpose risky trust into cognitive certitude,
that we have invested too much in packaged truth that has no transformative energy.
Forgive us, so that we may be your risk runners,
your promise trusters,
your future formers,
that we may not flinch from the costs of dreaming,
or the inconvenience of caring.
We have our days of doubt,
but then we see your newness
and receive your energy for lives that matter.
We gladly answer to your summons,
that we also may walk,

not by what we see,
but by what we know and hear from your life-giving lips.

We too are among those who live "by faith,"
by our wager on your good futures. Amen.

G is for Gottwald

We give thanks for Norman,

for his life of prophetic courage,

for his honest scholarship,

for his irenic spirit,

for his readiness to learn from others and to change his mind,

for his daring transformation of our discipline, and

for his indefatigable resolve in the service of justice.

We give thanks

for his towering intellect and his vast learning,

for his masterful book *The Tribes of Yahweh,*

that changed our course of study and understanding,

for his patient probes of historical questions,

for his ready contributions to our common interpretive enterprise,

for his shrewd discernment of social power and effective ideology, and

for his brave capacity to permit his study to touch our contemporaneity.

We are grateful for the major sociologists who have instructed Norman,
for Max Weber who probed the interface of religion and economics,
for Émile Durkheim who taught us to appreciate the generative force of community,
especially for Norman's recovery of Karl Marx
with his dialectical materialism and his attentiveness to the class struggle all around us.
We are grateful for the restless students at Berkeley
who were Norman's students,
and his teachers!
We give thanks for his close attentiveness to your character,
and his recognition that you always travel
with an egalitarian economics
and never without it,
that you are a source of social power,
and an impetus for social upheaval in the service of justice.
We are glad to affirm in your presence
the ways in which our work and
our faith and
our lives have been impacted by and altered by Norman's good work,

that we are able to see our money zones
as venues for social intervention, and
an alternative economy of neighborly justice is always on offer
because of your mighty resolve.
We thank you for Norman's careful critique of our great combines of wealth and power,
and the way in which he could imagine differently;
he is, in your wake, a source of hope for us,
a goad for our ongoing responsibility, and
an assurance for our enlistment in the work of justice.
And now, concerning his legacy,
we pledge to do the work he identified,
to do the critical analysis of our greedy exploitative status quo,
to do the generative work of alternative,
to do critical analysis and generative work with an imaginative spirit,
in confidence that the work we do is in the service of and in the train of your good will.
We finish with our embrace of the struggle for human liberation,
in the certain knowledge that the structures and forces of monopoly are stubborn and insistent,

but must finally yield to your good purpose
when performed with resolved, unflinching human nerve.
All praise to you, the liberator!
All gratitude for good scholarship that evokes our best thinking,
and our clearest vision of the world you are calling into being.
Amen.

H is for Holiness

We know the scene well:
    your majestic throne room
        filled with lively angelic agents,
        all gathered around your throne,
        busy with praise for you,
            love for you, and
            care for you.
All of them loudly, gladly singing:
    Holy,
    Holy twice,
    Holy three times,
        "Holy, holy, holy" everywhere always.
Their singing recognizes how unlike us you are,
            how deeply different,
            how incommensurate you are from all your creation.
We join their singing: "Holy, holy, holy."
We dare to sing you "Ancient of Days,"
    the one from of old—before all time,

through all time,
ordering all your creation for goodness and
peaceableness.
We dare to sing you the son
the poor, weak, foolish man of Nazareth,
the one who fills the hungry with good things,
and sends the rich empty away.
We dare to sing you Spirit,
the unshackled force who surges with new life,
who empowers us beyond ourselves,
who does the transformative work of making all things new,
just when we have resigned in fatigue and despair.
We do not understand your math
of three, of one,
of one in three,
of three in one;
but we sing three times holy
in recognition that you are all at once many and one;
We dare to extend your singular holiness
to the worldly realities that are freighted with your force:
We name holy places,
the venues of your peculiar presence,
the places of your sacraments,

the spots for facing your demanding presence.
We name holy times,
the Sabbath you blessed at the outset,
the great festal times of Yom Kippur and Rosh Hashanah
and Passover,
Christmas, Easter, and Pentecost,
times when your holiness has singularly permeated
our life in the world.
We name holy persons,
variously the ordained types of pastors and bishops,
and more compellingly the saints,
who give themselves away in vulnerability
for the sake of needful humanity.
In our seeking for assurance and certitude,
we go beyond holy places, holy times, and holy persons;
we mange inventories for holy living,
lists that too readily become catalogs that serve to exclude
the disqualified.

It boggles our thinking to know that your holiness
takes the form of justice and righteousness,
that you intend your world to be ordered for well-being,
and against our willful control.

It defies our best explanations that you in your holiness
are the primal practitioner of
faithfulness, steadfast love, and mercy,
that you, in your holiness stand alongside
widows, orphans, and immigrants,
that you invest yourself in places of hurt, need, and abuse,
that you finally submitted to the force of empire,
and died a brutal death.
We have watched your holiness descend upon us in solidarity,
as your strength has come as weakness,
as your wisdom has come as foolishness,
as your richness has come as poverty.
You are beyond our understanding,
as you are not contained in our explanations.
For that reason, we can only join the song of praise;
we can only echo the angels:
"Holy, holy, holy."
At the edge of our knowledge,
we must stop our control
and end—toward you,
lost in wonder, love, and praise. Amen.

I is for Irenic

We have it on your best authority:

"Blessed are the peacemakers,"

the ones who belong singularly to you.

The aphorism affirms that you, the God we worship, wills peace.

You are the God who anticipates, via Isaiah, a messiah who will be prince of peace,

who, on the lips of Jesus, ordered the storm to be ordered in peace,

who anticipated, via Micah, weapons of war transposed into agricultural tools,

swords into plowshares,

spears into pruning hooks;

who issued, via Aaron, our most trusted benediction,

"and give you peace."

Peace is a mighty intention for you, creator God.

But then the affirmation recognizes as well, that

peace is also a human task,

work to be done,

the work of compassion and honesty,
of truth-telling candor,
of unflinching respect for the other so unlike us.
We who are children and heirs of the German Evangelical tradition,
the tradition of my tribe of pietists,
may give great thanks that "irenic" is the key marker of the tradition from the outset;
it is a tradition that has shunned theological controversy,
that has refused theological hair-splitting, and
that has trusted the faithful intent of our Lutheran and Calvinist inheritance,
but that did not adjudicate between them.

We may be glad, in this tradition,
for pastors who understood the to-and-fro of human interaction,
who have been content to tone down controversy for the sake of shared well-being.
And now—among us—has come
a very different spirit,
a ruthless inclination to divide, defeat, and dominate.
We have arrived at a plateau
where liberals and conservatives refuse to live well together,
where liberals dismiss conservatives as lowlifes,
where conservatives regard liberals as traitors and heretics,

and "there is no health in us."
That toxic either/or so divides us
that your church teems with exclusionary fervor,
so that we drift toward self-assertive homogeneity,
all the while dismissing "the other" into the darkness.

It is no wonder that the early apostles are alert to the gift and the task of peace:

> The fruit of the Spirit is love, joy, peace . . . (Galatians)
>
> Keep on doing what you have learned and received and heard and seen in me, and the God of peace will be with you. (Philippians)
>
> And let the peace of Christ rule in your hearts, to which indeed you were called in the one body. And be thankful. (Colossians)
>
> Now may the Lord of peace himself give you peace at all times in all ways. (2 Thessalonians)
>
> Grace to you and peace from God our Father and the Lord Jesus Christ. (Philemon 3)
>
> May grace and peace be yours in abundance. (1 Peter)
>
> Grace, mercy, and peace will be with you from God the Father and from Jesus Christ, the Father's Son, in truth and love. (2 John 3)

The church, when it is quarrelsome, contradicts the good news entrusted to it.
For that reason, "quarrels, dissensions, factions" are reckoned to be "desires of the flesh,"
the sorry need to dominate and control.
We know better!
We know otherwise!
We in the church are called to be unlike that fearful world,
at peace amid a world in dispute,
at peace unlike the world that specializes in violence and destruction,
at peace, confident that all our disputes are penultimate to your good well.
In the end, we are blessed by you, the God of all peace,
who offers us peace that defies and that surpasses all our human understanding.
We may pray to you, the God of such peace,
that you will guard our hearts and minds,
that we may not fall into the poison of our fearful society,
that we may maintain a readiness to be led beyond our pet ideologies,
into reconciliations that are of your making,
into new friendships grounded in mutual good faith, and

into restorations that go beyond our hurts and
grudges.

Imagine:

Peacemaking is the performance of your good purpose!
Healing and restoration
grounded in truth-telling and forgiveness
are glad gospel gestures entrusted to us.

We pray this in the name of the peace-making, peace-governing, peace-willing God
who intends "heavenly well-being" here and now. Amen.

J is for Jeremiah

We give you thanks for Jeremiah,
    the man, the memory, the testimony, the book.
We thank you that you called him
    to his abrasive, buoyant utterance
    that rings with profound contemporaneity for us.
We thank you that early on
    he came to see your covenant as the only viable future for his
    people,
        to affirm your commandments the norm for public life in
        his city.
We thank you that he found courage and resolve
    to do the work of *plucking up and tearing down*
        even of our citadel of chosenness.
He did the required dismantling
    by his anticipation and declaration of war before it happened;
    by his deep imagery of plunges into death and chaos,
    by his acted parables of failure,
    by his articulation of love betrayed as whoredom,

by his recognition of drought as a work of our undoing, and
by his exposure of false assurances that contradicted reality.
We attend to his grief as he anticipated the death of his city,
as he summoned Israel in sorrow to turn and to change,
as he wept in regret over the loss he knew was coming,
as he found silence impossible, and so his plaintive voice.
We are glad that he did not stop at fearsome judgment from you.
We thank you that he found a second wind and a second awareness,
to do the work of *planting and building*,
hosting a new future through his images and poetic cadences.

We thank you for his second version of new possibility,
for his anticipation of our new covenant for his people
grounded in forgiveness and your generous forgetfulness.
for his glad belated welcome of a king to come
filled with righteousness and justice,
the realities of old covenantal purposes,
for his courageous expectation of the collapse of long-running menacing superpower,
for his readiness to have mother Rachel's weeping come to an end,
for his wondrous confidence in the certitude of your gracious, good rule.
We thank you for this brave, imagination-filled speaker of your truth,

and for the scribes who preserved his words
and ordered his book,
so that his grieving honesty is available to us,
so that we may participate in his anguished truth telling of a world gone amuck,
so that we may participate in his deep grief over the loss of what we have treasured;
so that we may linger with him in hope-filled possibility beyond present circumstance.
We give thanks for the train of his followers who echo his truth,
for those who refuse to leave our skewed world in its complacent indifference,
for those who insist upon our new world so poignantly on offer among us.
We give thanks for Jesus of Nazareth,
who followed closely in his wake,
who took up the work of *plucking up and tearing down*,
in his *death and execution*;
who lived out the work of *planting and building*
in his *Easter resurrection*.
We thank you for this urgent truth telling as you preside
over even our most treasured arrangements,
as you judge our ready contradiction of your good purposes,

as you generate newness even amid our recalcitrance,
as you remain at the good work of bringing our world to your good sense.

We thank you that you have not left us without prophetic witness even now;

give us willing hearts to heed;
give us the freedom to relinquish what has failed;
give us receptive hearts to receive your newness,
give us openness to your governance that refuses to leave us in our deception.

Our hope, like that of Jeremiah, is in none other,
save in you alone. Amen.

K IS FOR KNOWLEDGE OF GOD

John Calvin opens *The Institutes of Christian Living* with these famous words:

> Without knowledge of self there is no knowledge of God. Nearly all the wisdom we possess, which is to say, true and sound wisdom, consists in two parts, a knowledge of God and of ourselves.

To this Calvin adds:

> Without knowledge of God there is no knowledge of self.
> Piety is a requisite for the knowledge of God.
> Knowledge of God involves trust and reverence.

We come to you, God beyond all our knowing, with eagerness to know you more fully.
We thank you that you instruct us concerning yourself,
that you show yourself to us.
In your primary emancipatory tale, we have come to know you:
By this you shall know that I am the Lord. (Exodus 7:17)

So that you may know that there is no one like the Lord our God. (Exodus 8:10)

. . . that you may know I the Lord am in this land. (Exodus 8:22)

. . . so that you may know that there is none like me in all earth. (Exodus 8:14)

. . . so that you may know that the earth is the Lord's. (Exodus 9:20)

. . . so that you may know that I am the Lord. (Exodus 10:2)

. . . then you shall know that I am the Lord your God. (Exodus 16:12)

We know you in your emancipatory action,

in your overthrow of Pharaoh's slave system,

in your dismantling of exploitative social systems.

We know you alongside the Egyptians, recipients of your harsh self-disclosure amid their power:

The Egyptians shall know that I am the Lord. (Exodus 7:5)

The Egyptians shall know that I am the Lord. (Exodus 14:4)

The Egyptians shall know that I am the Lord. (Exodus 14:18)

We do not know you as an idea or as a concept;

we know you as an active agent in the life of your world,

as one who takes sides in the social struggle,

as one who adjudicates economic matters on behalf
of the vulnerable,
you, who are restless with exploitation and mean-spirited
greed.
We give thanks to you for ancient Jeremiah who saw clearly
that knowing you is found in the enactment of
justice for the poor,
who understood that your hidden self is made
evident to us
in advocacy for the poor and needy.
We can thus imagine a wholesome exchange between
ancient Jeremiah,
and bold Calvin,
a conversation to which we may be privy,
an exchange that resists empty syllogistic
formulation,
and sees that you are available to us
precisely in the struggle for justice as nowhere
else.
Given this reality of our knowledge,
we ask for forgiveness,
for our excessive preoccupation with intellectual
formulation,

for our overinvestment in ideas that keep you
remote from our daily reality,
for our pursuit of certitude concerning you,
when you are the God who calls us to deep risk.
We are grateful for our ancient sages,
who taught us that the "fear of you" is the root of all our wisdom,
fear that takes you with utmost seriousness,
fear that becomes awe before you,
fear that turns to glad obedience and willing trust.
We are caught up short when the apostle juxtaposes knowledge to love.
In our modern world we have bet everything on knowledge,
seeing that knowledge is power,
trusting that knowledge will supply our needs,
that technology is the way to self-sufficiency.
Amid our modern sense of mastery through knowledge,
we are sobered by
love of your self-giving kind—*agape*:
love that is patient,
love that is kind,
love that is not envious or boastful or arrogant or rude,

love that does not seek its own way,
love that bears all things,
believes all things,
hopes all things,
endures all things,
love that never ends;
And then knowledge
that does not love!
We pray that we may let our knowledge be fully permeated by your love,
that we may trust that our knowledge is best when it begins in your self-giving,
that we may embrace our knowledge,
our scientific capacity,
our technological capability,
as qualified, shaped, and enhanced by your *agape*.
Grant that we may know you more fully,
as we witness to your emancipatory governance.
We know you now in part, but then we shall know you fully,
even as we are known. Amen.

L IS FOR LAMENT

You are the God from whom no secret is hid,
even if we would like to hide something of ourselves from you.
You are the God to whom all hearts are open,
even when we choose hard-heartedness;
You are the God who hears and answers our prayers before we utter them.
You are the God who is like a mother who answers before we call.
For these reasons, we pray often and easily:
We pray prayers of thanks,
especially at mealtimes,
ready to acknowledge "that all good gifts are sent from heaven above."
We pray lavish prayers of praise,
all the way from great choral offerings to the simplest of "praise hymns."
We pray prayers of petition,
seeking your response to our needs and fears.
We pray prayers of intercession,
holding before you our neighbors in need.

What we do not do easily or well
is to utter laments that bespeak
our losses, our hurts, our grievances, and our angers.
We do not utter laments,
because they seem unworthy of us,
as inappropriate before you,
because we think that mostly we can and must manage on our own,
because we doubt your capacity to respond effectively to our deep need.
We do not utter lament,
and so we engage in denial before you concerning our lives;
we withhold the deep truth of our lives from you.
In our more sober moments, nevertheless,
we are glad that we belong to a great company of those who boldly spoke lament to you:
we thank you for Moses,
who vigorously protested your intent to destroy;
we thank you for Jeremiah, who voiced his anguished need directly to you;
we thank you for Job,
who refused to be silenced by his well-meaning friends;
we thank you for Jesus,
who on the night of his arrest by the authorities,

quoted the old Psalm,
and voiced his awareness of your abandonment of him,
as you left him alone in his risk.
We thank you for this great company of lamenters
who called out in their circumstances of need,
who accepted that you would listen,
who let their laments spill over into complaint and protest and demand,
calling you to account for your inattentiveness.
We pray the courage and honesty,
to utter our deep hurt-filled truth before you.
Hear us, as we voice our fear for our public life under assault.
Hear us as we face the violence of our society,
with its mad nationalism,
its uncurbed racism, and
its craven sexism.
Hear us as we monitor the abusive demise of our natural environment,
as we imagine that our technology can save us.
Hear us as we cringe before the passing of an old world
with its proper reliable order,
with its stable church,
with its assured humanity,
and now a context becomes odd and strange, and ominous.

We are left, as we speak our truth,
with the old long-running wonderment
of Moses, of Jeremiah, of Job,
Do you know?
Do you notice?
Do you care?
We end our prayers with a rote "amen":
but we wonder and we wait;
we wait with eager longing,
and you seem in no hurry to answer.
Hear us as we make utterance to you,
as we pray the deepest of our prayers:
Save us!
Save us from ourselves;
save his from our fears;
save us from our power;
save us from our pride.
Save us, that we may sing our lives back to you,
in praise and thanks and wonderment. Amen.

M is for Moses

Moses looms so large in the text and in the tradition
    that we can scarcely find adequate words for him.
We give you thanks for Moses,
    and for all that he embodies.
We thank you for his great authority as an intrepid *liberator*:
    he risked to confront Pharaoh;
    he dared to insist upon emancipation of the slaves of the empire;
    he stood toe-to-toe with imperial technocrats and by your power bested them;
    he watched as your powers of chaos did their mighty work;
    he ended his liberating work by his buoyant singing
        when he affirmed your capacity to reorder the world.
    We thank you for the inventory of revolutions that have followed his lead,
        for the French revolution that brought democracy into the world;
        for the US revolution that ended taxation without representation;

for the Russian revolution that ended imperialism,
for the Chinese revolution that recognized the severe needs of peasants.
All these upheavals in the wake of Moses and his freedom!
We thank you for his skill as a *covenant-maker*,
as he stood in the midst of your awesome presence,
as he gathered nameless, stateless people and created new community;
as he fearlessly negotiated between your uncompromising governance
and the recurring waywardness of his new community;
as he imagined a covenant community
distinct from collective authoritarianism
and from isolated individualism;
as he modeled democratic possibility
long before we had heard that word.
We thank you for *his fierce articulation of your commandments*,
his Big Two concerning love of you and love of neighbor,
for his elucidation of your will and purpose
for every aspect of our common life,
from food to work to worship to money, sexuality, and civic order,
for his unwavering conviction that obedience to you
is the sum of genuine freedom.

We thank you for *his capacity for daring prayer,*
for his readiness to pray boldly on behalf of his people,
for his capacity to enter your presence and confront you,
for his self-forgetting doxology before you.
We thank you that he became *the authorizer of our most treasured scripture,*
that his signature pervades all of Torah;
that he gave us not only your commands at Sinai,
but a "second version" in Deuteronomy,
that he specifies Torah as his comrade, Elijah, specifies prophecy,
as the two of them,
Moses and Elijah,
Torah and the prophets,
stood alongside Jesus on the holy mountain of transformation.
We thank you for all the brave company
of those who follow him, and
reiterate his passion for you and for your justice:
for the ancient prophets who echo his will to justice,
for the company of priests who seek to implement his call to holiness,
for Jesus of Nazareth who came to fulfill and make more radical his teaching,
for the great teachers of the church who repeat his cadences,

for stark prophetic voices who are unafraid,
for Savonarola who critiqued his self-indulgent elites,
for Wilberforce who labored long for freedom in the old empire,
for Frederick Douglas who performed his narrative of emancipation,
for Martin Luther King who lived toward the dream,
for William Barber who continues the great work of economic justice, and
for the great company of truth tellers who are embodied carriers of the gospel.

We thank you for the alternative world that Moses could imagine,
alternative to power from the top,
alternative to enslaving acquisitiveness,
alternative to monopoly and greed via shameless violence,
alternative to conquest and colonialization.

We thank you for the empowering legacy of Judaism that at its best echoes his cadences,
for the ways the Mosaic-Jewish cadences
have infiltrated Christian faith and Islamic conviction.

Moses and his fierce imperative
bespeak the phony failure of all our idols,
of class and race and gender and nation.

We are gladly bewitched by Moses's ongoing and endless
contemporaneity,
    how he himself declared:
        "Not with our ancestors did the Lord make this covenant,
        but with us, who are all of us here alive today!"
His emancipatory faith is alive among us here and now,
    always with us in our present circumstance,
    always with us in our specificity.
Give us, we pray, the freedom and courage and honesty
    to walk in his parade of faithful freedom,
    that we may stand—soon and late—
        with the vulnerable of the earth.
    Free at last,
        thank God almighty,
        free at last! Amen.

N IS FOR NATIONALISM

We are able to watch in amazement
as you gathered together
the lost, the rejected, the vulnerable, the disadvantaged,
the ones without hope or identity,
and formed them into a new people.
You heard their cry in bondage;
you gathered them, emancipated them, and formed them
into a new community
shaped for and by your good purposes.
You dared to designate them
a priestly kingdom,
a holy nation.
We observed as you kept your old promise of land
in this new convergence of property and power.
All—your wondrous blessing!
But then came a new dreaming of power,
a resolve to "be like the other nations,"
to imitate them in power, wealth, and grandeur.

You answered their request,
somewhere between lukewarm and rejection.
But Israel got its king as requested;
the new king acted like a king . . .
confiscated, usurped, possessed, and taxed,
until the peasants were desperate and revolted;
they refused the king's taxation!
But the kings persisted—
great palaces,
a great temple,
a great harem,
great commerce,
everything pressed to scale,
as the royal coveting knew no limits,
all exhibits of royal control.
You, in your resistance to such indulgence . . .
warned and protested—
you sent your bold prophets:
Amos who exposed the self-indulgent living;
Isaiah who observed monopolies of property with complementary displacement,
Micah who saw covenantal norms easily dismissed,
until Jeremiah

who could imagine the end of the state,
the loss of the capitol city,
the deportation of the royal family, and
the undoing of the royal temple apparatus.
It turned out that the great national ideology—
the claim of chosenness—was unsustainable.
It turned out that even this chosen nation
was subject to your will and commandment,
to justice that would not be mocked.
The chants of king and temple were no assurance in the face of
exploitative injustice;
and so the end,
the loss,
the displacement,
the weeping, and
the failure of a dreamed of immunity.
It followed:
your people recovered only modestly;
your holy city rebuilt only partially;
your temple restored, but not grandly;
we settled for status as a funded colony;
we rallied around your Torah,
to the disregard of temple, king, and city.

We share lingering hopes,
but in the meantime, we have reality to face;
we face it with tears,
and some hints of joyous well-being.
And now us, in the United States!
With our memory of being your newly chosen people,
with our claim to a new land of promise,
with our reassurances as your blessed community,
all of which we have squandered in arms,
in aggressive commerce,
in white privilege at the cost of well-being for people of color,
to the disadvantage of the lowly among us.
We—like your ancient chosen people,
stand convicted of using our chosenness
for self-regard and self-sufficiency, and self-congratulations.
And we end . . . at risk,
at risk of your rejection,
at risk of being overwhelmed by enemies we have created,
at risk in our cocoon of illusion.
We prattle all day long about our chosenness,
of being the land of the free and the home of the brave;
but at night it does not feel so much like freedom

or like bravery,
but only vulnerability.
At midnight we are filled with some shame
and some guilt,
and some bewilderment
about our future,
about your purpose for us, and
about our way forward,
whether more wealth, power, and wisdom
or perhaps
more justice, righteousness, and mercy.
You pose hard choices for us,
and we pray and probe, and puzzle. Amen.

O IS FOR OMRI

Why, you may well ask, Omri? After all
he was the king in Northern Israel for only *eight years*;
he receives only *thirteen verses* in the royal account of the book of Kings,
an account that consists in condemnation for the evil he did.
Other than a couple genealogical mentions,
he gets only a condemnation from Micah, the prophet.
That is all . . . So why bother with him?
For all his failure and condemnation,
he founded a royal dynasty that lasted for four generations;
he is mentioned in the Assyrian Chronicles by name;
he had an important international reputation as a trader;
he knew how to buy and sell and ship and trade,
all to his monetary advantage.
He was in his time a force to be reckoned with,
who left a large footprint in his time and place.
Read through the lens of Israel's faith in YHWH,
here are three factors to consider:

First, Omri enjoyed an international reputation as a trader;
he would not permit his Israelite singularity to get in the way of his economic prowess.
He brought great wealth to his realm,
and to his new capital city of Samaria with its famous "ivories."
Second, he must have found YHWH, the God of covenantal neighborliness, to be an
impediment to his accumulation.
The rules of Yahwism offered preferences, obligations, and mandates that contradicted
his unfettered pursuit of trade and money.
Third, consequently Omri had to tone down Yahwism;
he did so with a blatant embrace of Baalism,
the Canaanite religion growth, generativity, and production.
Thus he joined issue as a practitioner of Baalism,
a commitment that culminated in the dramatic contest
of YHWH and Baal at Mount Carmel during the time of his son, Ahab.
It required the fierce prophet Elijah to enunciate clearly the deep either/or
that Israel faced in its religious practice.

Omri had no hesitation about his choice: it was Baal!
His dynasty prospered under Baal,
until it did not,
as it ended in bloodbath caused by religious conservatives.
Thus with *eight years* and *thirteen verses*
we have this shrewd model of economic predation
dominant in his time and place,
legitimated by the god of growth.
We may imagine
that if King Omri had had a moment of sober reflection
amid his great success,
perhaps late in his life,
he might have been a candidate for prayer and repentance.
We might imagine how he would assert his confession before
YHWH, the God whom he had deserted:
We confess that we have sinned against you
in thought, word, and deed,
by what we have done,
and by what we have left undone.
We have no evidence that Omri did this; but he might have!

So it may be with us and among us:
Not unlike Omri

- we have gone down the path of aggressive acquisitive commerce,

  dominating the world economy,

  using up world resources, and many peoples of the world.
- we have failed the mandate of the biblical gospel,

  finding neighborliness to be an inconvenience,

  that we have scuttled or

  readily transposed into an aberrant missional zeal concerning money and power;
- we have embraced a generic god of consumption, growth, and accumulation,

  all grounded in the god of white supremacy and exploitation.

We have eagerly, even if unwittingly, reperformed the ways of Omri:

with Omri the rejection of YHWH frees for exploitation of neighbors;

so with us, wealthy white America has had no reservation about exploitation,

unchecked by any gospel mandate toward our neighbor.

We might imagine, as we imagine with Omri, a confession of sin

for the way we have skewed the history of our time.

We might indeed imagine how the king might have prayed and how we might in turn pray:

By what we have done.

What we have done is to use up world resources as well as defenseless populations;

By what we have left undone.

We have left undone love of neighbor, provision for the needy, protection of the vulnerable, respect for the neighbor unlike us;

We have not loved you with our whole heart;

We have found it easier and more attractive to worship the "God of America"

who does not impose such hard commands.

We have not loved our neighbor as ourselves;

We have imagined that the neighbor has no claim upon us.

All of this is to impose too much on King Omri;

but then it may be

that for all our greedy consumption

that all we will get

is *eight years* and *thirteen verses* in the Book of Life.

Life is short when lived against the grain of the real Lord of our lives.

When we face the reality of our common life,

we might receive more years and more verses in the Book of Life. Amen.

P is for Prayer

In the catechism of my youth, we get this:

> Prayer is the conversation of the heart with God for the purpose of praising him, asking him to supply the needs of ourselves and others, and thanking him for whatever he gives. (*Evangelical Catechism*, p. 59, #101)

In *The Heidelberg Catechism*, the question is posed in this way:

> Why is prayer necessary for Christians?

And the answer goes like this:

> Because it is the chief part of the gratitude which God requires of us, and because God gives his grace and Holy Spirit only to those who sincerely beseech him in prayer without ceasing, and who thank him for these gifts. (*The Heidelberg Catechism*, p. 116, #116)

Prayer is a conversation of gratitude with the giver of all good gifts.

Prayer is the affirmation that our lives are penultimate,
derivative from the goodness of God,
to be lived back to God in glad obedience.

Prayer is an active performance of a lively interaction
that defines our life in the world,
as our life gratefully before God.
That lively conversation with God involves:
Praise that bespeaks the wonder, magnitude, and splendor of God;
Thanks that recognizes God as the giver of all good gifts,
for we know that we have nothing that has not been given to us;
Asking,

- both for ourselves in our neediness (petition),
- for the neediness of our neighbors (intercession).

Of these several elements, Karl Barth judges that the most
definitional and elemental is "simply asking."
It is asking that marks the immense incommensurability
between us and the Holy Giver who makes our life possible.
"Simply asking" acknowledges our dependence and reliance upon the goodness of God.
We may imagine two conditions in which prayer becomes impossible:

- prayer is impossible in our self-sufficiency, when we imagine we can be on our own;

• prayer is impossible in the depth of despair when
we sink into immobilizing oblivion.

"Simply asking" is an antidote to both of these conditions:
"simply asking" is a direct contradiction to self-sufficiency;
"simply asking" is an alternative to our abandonment,
an insistence on being taken seriously,
a refusal to the thought that we are abandoned.

Once we have "simply asked,"
we may extend our asking:
• we may recognize our needs and hopes are greater than
we had at first imagined, and so
our asking becomes more urgent;
• we may recognize that as we ask for ourselves,
we can ask for our neighbors as well,
seeking that the Holy God will supply for our
neighbors what is needed.

Asking may speak in many voices:
It may come in the serenity of confident prayer;
It may come in the grudging imperatives of doubt;
It may come in the shrillness of abandonment;
so it was with our ancestors,
the slaves under Pharaoh.
It is said of them only that they "groaned and cried out."

The text does not say that they cried out to anyone in particular,
or that their groan was addressed to anyone.
Their groan and cry was more elemental,
a bodily ache that required expression.

The wonder of their groan and cry
is that it rose up to God;
it went to its proper destination,
for this is the God—the one we confess to be the only God—
functions like a magnet for our deepest groans and our most shrill cries.
Their inchoate prayer comes to fruition when it is affirmed:
God heard,
God remembered,
God saw,
God took notice . . .
God came down to save.
The conversation is complete.
Israel in its need has *asked*;
God, in God's goodness, has *answered*.
The prayers of Israel over time grew longer and more ornate.
The praise of Israel became eloquent and expansive;

the thanks of Israel developed a long inventory of specificities;

but at bottom Israel's prayer—and so the prayer of the church—

is about asking.

We can observe the asking of Israel:

in the royal prayer of David: "May it continue forever before you";

in the temple prayer of Solomon: "Hear in heaven";

in the prophetic petition of Amos: "Forgive, he is so small";

in the desperate prayer of King Hezekiah: "O Lord God, save us";

in the needy prayer of Jeremiah: "Let me see your retribution upon them."

The great tradition of Israel's prayer comes to Christian culmination

in the prayer of Jesus that we style "The Lord's Prayer."

The prayer is filled with petitions:

for bread, for forgiveness, for deliverance,

and it ends in a grand doxology.

Prayer is the alternative of faith,

enough to refuse self-sufficiency

in which we do not dare to ask or even imagine our need;
enough to forego our deepest abandonment in which we see ourselves beyond help.
So now, let us resolve that we,
the company of those who trust the gospel,
be regularly,
without fail,
disciplined and daring in our asking.
We may pray for courage and stamina to perform our faith;
We may pray for blessing upon the good work of justice and peace;
We may pray for transformation,
that we are delivered from predatory violence;
We may pray that beyond all our coping capacity,
God will be effectively at work
to restore our world to well-being in our obedient freedom.
Our prayers—soon or late—affirm that to God
not to our nation,
not to our race,
not to our gender,
not to us
belong the kingdom, the power and the glory. Amen.

Q IS FOR QUICK

In the King James Version (KJV) of the Bible, Psalm 119 is replete with the word *quick* in the sense of "being alive." The psalm is a meditation on God's Torah and the resolve of the psalmist to live faithfully according to the commands of Torah. The psalm is artistically constructed with an eight-fold acrostic, that is, it works its way through the Hebrew alphabet so that the first eight lines of the psalm begin with *aleph*, the first letter of the Hebrew alphabet, all the way through to *taw*, that is, from *A* to *Z*. The point of such artistry is to assert the fullness and completeness of Torah as a guide for a faithful life. Unfortunately, all this remarkable artistry is lost in translation. We may nonetheless take note of this work of artistic completeness. Everything is accounted for. The Torah envelopes all of life; every sphere of our lives is under the domain and imperative of the creator God.

It is especially important to notice that the psalm never suggests that obedience to Torah merits the gift of life. This is not "works' righteousness." Rather the psalmist fully understands and affirms that life is itself a gift from God, a gift that is to be lived in obedience to God.

In the course of the psalm in the KJV the term "quick" occurs eleven times:

> *Quicken thou me according to thy word. (v. 25)*
>
> *Quicken thou me in thy way. (v. 37)*
>
> *Quicken me in thy righteousness. (v. 40)*

> *Thy word hath quickened me. (v. 50)*
> *Quicken me after thy loving kindness. (v. 88)*
> *With them ("thy precepts") thou hast quickened me. (v. 93)*
> *Quicken me according to thy word. (v. 107)*
> *Quicken me according to thy judgment. (v. 149)*
> *Quicken me according to thy word. (v. 154)*
> *Quicken me according to thy judgments. (v. 156)*
> *Quicken me, O Lord, according to thy loving kindness. (v. 159)*

Nine times the verb "quicken" is an imperative addressed to God. Twice it is an acknowledgement of God's completed quickening work. In all cases, the trigger for "quickening" is a dimension of God's fidelity, variously named as "judgment," "loving kindness," "precepts," "righteousness," "way," and "word." Each of these is an articulation of God's capacity for relational empowerment. The term *quicken* refers to vitality, energy, liveliness, all received as a gift from God, the giver of life. For those of us who find this usage a bit odd, we may notice a more familiar and more conventional usage in the Apostles' Creed:

> From thence he shall come to judge *the quick* and the dead.

That is, God presides over the living and the dead, all human creatures in the sphere of the earth. The formula, "quick and dead" attests that the creator God is the Lord of all life; nothing falls outside God's providential care.

We may grasp the force of "quick" in the KJV usage when we see how the term is rendered, for example, in the New Revised Standard Version (NRSV):

> Revive me *according to your word. (v. 25)*
> Give me life *in your ways. (v. 37)*
> *In your righteousness* give me life. *(v. 40)*
> . . . *that your promise* gives me life. *(v. 50)*
> *In your steadfast love* spare my life. *(v. 88)*
> *By them (your precepts) you have* given me life. *(v. 93)*
> Give me life, *O Lord, according to your word. (v. 107)*
> *O Lord, in your justice* preserve my life. *(v. 149)*
> Give me life *according to your promise. (v. 154)*
> Give me life *according to your justice. (v. 156)*
> Preserve my life *according to your steadfast love. (v. 159)*

In each case the governing verb is a verbal form of *hyh*, life, that is, give life. Thus, the NRSV renders as some form of "give life," whereas the KJV prefers "quicken." Either way, life is seen to be the gift of YHWH and life is the hope of the psalmist.

In the NRSV, the agency of YHWH is reiterated as in the KJV, and rendered as "justice," "precept," "promise," "righteousness," "steadfast love," "way," and "word" the same terms as in the KJV with a somewhat different translation. Each of these terms bespeaks YHWH's attentive, generative fidelity. The psalmist never doubts that YHWH, as lord of life, can and will rescue us from the zone of death; this is the claim, whether we take the absolute zone of death, or whether we refer to the many ways of weakness and diminishment that beset our lives. Either way, YHWH is *the giver*, Israel is *the hoper.*

The mood of the Psalm is one of sober humanity that recognizes that being "quick" depends upon the generous intent of YHWH, the life-giver. Without that life-giver, there can be no quickness, but only a failed shell of existence at best.

We may recognize, via the psalmist, that the well-being of "quickness" does not consist in money, power, or wisdom. It consists, rather, in the relational quality of covenant. It is this relationship with YHWH that makes our quickness possible, a quickness that extends inescapably to our neighborly interactions as well. Thus, the Torah of Israel affirms that neighborliness is the extension of quickness to neighbors who may themselves have lost their capacity for life. It is a marvel that covenantal existence may indeed bestow *quickness* on our neighbors, as it can upon us.

Thus we may pray with the psalmist:
Without you, we are left to invent quickness on our own;
with you we gladly receive your gift of quickness.
We pledge to live out our quickness that we have from you
in response to your summons to obedience,
by extending our quickness in and for and on behalf of our neighborhood. Amen.

R is for von Rad

Gerhard von Rad (1901–1971)

—with his erudition, his eloquence, and his courage,

was likely the most important scholar of Old Testament

Theology in the twentieth century.

From the outset of my work, he has been my lodestar for my scholarship.

My seminary teacher, Lionel Whiston, had introduced me to his work,

as we read von Rad's *Studies in Deuteronomy*,

a work in which he articulates the dynamism of the Torah

endlessly reiterated as "preached law."

As a young scholar at the University of Jena during the war years and the Nazis,

he was the only member of the theology faculty of the university who was not a Nazi.

As a result, he had no students—

except those Bonhoeffer sent him from his seminary in the Confessing Church.

In his early days von Rad published two astonishing articles:

In 1936, "The Theological Problem of the Old Testament Doctrine of Creation."[1]

Von Rad equated Canaanite religion to Nazi ideology and saw that, as a result, "creation" could not be the defining mark of Israel's covenant.

In 1938, "The Form-Critical Problem of the Hexateuch."[2]

He explored the several traditions of the "Hexateuch" and

saw that together they explicated Israel's "credo"

through which Israel articulated its singular Yahwism

that would withstand the challenge of Canaanite religion.

In both essays von Rad saw the immediate contemporaneity of these traditions

for his own German context vis-à-vis the Nazis.

He refused "creation theology" that tilted toward "fertility religion" and thus to "German soil."

He asserted the "credo" of Israel as standing ground against the Nazis.

In his middle years,

von Rad published his two-volume *Old Testament Theology*:

volume 1 is largely an exposition of his Hexateuchal study;

---

[1] See *The Problem of the Hexateuch and Other Essays* (McGraw-Hill, 1966), 131–143.

[2] See *The Problem of the Hexateuch and Other Essays*, 1–78.

volume 2 is an exploration of the prophetic tradition;
He linked the two volumes by an appeal to Isaiah 43:18–19:
Do not remember the former things,
or consider the things of old.
I am about to do a new thing;
now it springs forth, do you not perceive it?
He understood "former things" to be the Hexateuchal memory,
and the "new thing" as the new world of prophetic anticipation.
Most remarkably, near the end of his life
he published *Wisdom in Israel*, a book that is nothing short of a third volume in his *Old Testament Theology*.
In that volume von Rad explicated the wisdom tradition of Israel:
he sees the defining link to Near Eastern wisdom teaching, and
he sees that wisdom theology is an exploration of creation theology.
Thus late in his life, in his quite new context,
he recognized an opening to creation theology
that he had, in an earlier context, rejected.
It is surely a part of von Rad's generative capacity that he would,
late in his life,
reverse his position, and
take a new path that was both permitted and required by his new interpretive context.

My own exposure to the magisterial work of von Rad includes:

my first reading of his study of Deuteronomy in seminary;

in my graduate study, von Rad's impact was not yet felt, but he did make one trip to the United States;

I heard him lecture one time at Union Seminary;

on my first sabbatical leave in 1970, I studied in Heidelberg

that was at the time the "headquarters" for the most generative Old Testament study.

Von Rad, along with his all-star colleagues, Claus Westermann and Hans Walter Wolff,

had generated a remarkable series of graduate students,

many of whom became distinguished professors in their own right.

During my sabbatical year

I heard von Rad preach in the University Church

I attended the faculty Old Testament seminar where he was the all-star,

I once had coffee with him;

he was an overwhelming presence,

recognized by his contemporaries as an exceptional force and presence.

Along with Martin Noth, von Rad embodied the best of German Old Testament interpretation;

he was open to the playful artistry of the text;
this was quite in contrast to the positivistic tilt of US scholarship
that was largely enthralled by archeological discovery.
What struck me most about the work of von Rad
—that continues to strike me—
is his ready, easy capacity to do first rate scholarship (who could doubt it?)
while at the same time being deeply committed to its faith claims
voiced by the church.
For von Rad and his generation of German scholars in the Confessing Church,
there is no conflict between and no reason to choose between *scholarship* and *faith.*
We may indeed offer prayers of thanks for von Rad:
for his courage in a context of profound danger,
for his style that verged toward the poetic,
for his faith that was uncompromising,
for his erudition in which he was singularly generative of new readings, and
for his modesty of presence that gives gravitas to his work.
We may continue our prayers beyond him: prayers of hope:

that God will in time to come, generate scholars who witness to faith,

that God will bless the church with sound learning,

that God summon pastors and church leaders who remain grounded in these old texts, and

that the church may perform its life with courage and stamina in the hard days ahead.

Two reference points stand out for me in the work of von Rad:

he returned always again to Deuteronomy with its dynamic of faith

being endlessly reiterated afresh, and

the appreciation of "the new thing" grounded in Isaiah 43.

We may, alongside the discernment of von Rad

be vigilant for the "new thing" that God is doing among us, that summons us

—as he was summoned—

beyond what is old, settled, and taken for granted.

Von Rad understood that God's good promises

are always on their way to fresh fulfillment. Amen.

S is for Scroll

Robert Alter has shrewdly observed that Judaism is

a "culture of interpretation";

Judaism lives by the endless production of new interpretations

of the old text,

both oral and written.

These new interpretations make clear the irresistible power of the old scroll to evoke

new historical reality,

new discernments of God's holiness, and

new embraces of Torah obedience.

Here are three compelling evidences of "scroll power":

A. It is recorded that the high Priest, Hilkiah, reported to Shaphan, the royal secretary,

"I have found the Book of the Torah in the house of the Lord" (2 Kings 22:8).

The scribe in turn read the scroll to King Josiah,

a scroll that scholarship concludes is some form of Deuteronomy.

Upon hearing the scroll with its commandments and its culminating blessings and curses,

King Josiah "tore his clothes," that is,

he engaged in a visible, physical act of repentance.

Josiah understood immediately that he and his regime

stood indicted and convicted by the scroll

and were subject to its harsh judgment.

The narrative continues to report that King Josiah

instituted a great *religious* reform of his realm.

We are able to see, moreover, that his religious reform

had immense *political and economic* implications.

His contemporary, Jeremiah, remembers that the king made provision for the needy and poor (22:15–16).

By contrast it is narrated that when the ominous prophetic scroll of Jeremiah

was read to the son of Josiah, King Jehoiakim,

the king reacted by cutting the scroll in pieces and

throwing it into his fireplace (Jeremiah 36:23),

his attempt to silence and dismiss the scroll.

His defiant, dismissive action led to a harsh prophetic condemnation of the king,

fating him to the Babylonian invasion and the end of the dynasty.

King Josiah understood the dangerous, generative force of the scroll;
his son, Jehoiakim, understood nothing of the force of the scroll.

B. The narrative of the temptation of Jesus by the devil
reports that Jesus was tempted three times in three ways:

- a temptation to perform a miracle (Matthew 4, Luke 4:3),
- a temptation to worship the devil (Matthew 4:9, Luke 4:6), and
- a temptation to commit a spectacular life-risking jump (Matthew 4:6, Luke 4:9).

To each of these temptations Jesus makes a response from the old scroll of Deuteronomy:

- to the temptation to do a miracle he responds with Deuteronomy 8:3:

  One does not live by bread alone;
- to the temptation to worship the devil, he responds with Deuteronomy 6:4–5:

  To God, to our God, the Lord alone;
- to the temptation for a spectacular jump, he responds with Deuteronomy 6:16:

  Do not put the Lord your God to the test, as you tested him at Massah.

This set of texts yield for me an image of Jesus

—scroll in hand—

swatting the devil endlessly

until the devil retreats to "a more opportune time."

It takes only the scroll to fend off the power of evil!

C. Leviticus 25 attests the only clear reference to Jubilee in the Old Testament.

That chapter provides for

the cancelation of debt,

the restoration of property, and

the recovery of social viability.

Michael Hudson, *And Forgive Them Their Debts: Lending, Foreclosure and Redemption from Bronze Age Finance to the Jubilee Year* (2018) has offered compelling evidence that the practice of Jubilee as widespread in the ancient world!

It is quite remarkable that belated Isaiah,

after the exile,

should allude to this old text:

He has sent me to bring good news to the oppressed,

to bind up the brokenhearted,

to proclaim liberty to the captives, and release to the prisoners,

to proclaim the year of the Lord's favor (Isaiah 61:1–2).

This clear allusion to Jubilee anticipates that restored Israel, after the exile,

would practice an economy that is alternative to predation.

As close as we come to evidence for such an actual practice

is the action of Nehemiah, the Persian governor.

He saw that some Jews were exploiting other Jews

and took steps to remedy such usurpation.

He issued as stern and uncompromising imperative:

Restore to them this very day,

their fields, their vines, their livestock, and their houses, and the interest on money, grain, wine, and oil that you have been exacting from them (Nehemiah 5:11).

The predators readily accepted his imperative:

We will restore everything and demand nothing more from them.

We will do as you say (Nehemiah 5:12).

The old text continues its force into the narrative of Jesus.

In the Gospel of Luke, it is reported that Jesus in the synagogue

read from the text of Isaiah 61:

. . . He has sent me to proclaim release to the captives

and recovery of sight to the blind,

to let the oppressed go free,

to proclaim the year of the Lord's favor (Luke 4:18).

He declared the old practice of Jubilee to be in force present tense;
and then he scandalized the congregation with this:
"Today this scripture has been fulfilled in your hearing" (v. 21).
He himself is an agent of Jubilee,
of debt cancelation,
of restoration of property, and
of vitality for all members of the community.
In all three cases,
Josiah responding to the old scroll and repenting,
Jesus reiterating Deuteronomy to defeat the devil, and
Isaiah and Jesus appealing to the Jubilee text,
we see the continuing generative force and authority of the old text
through the memory of the community
and into the daring action of the community.
The scroll only requires a community
that treasures it,
that heeds it,
that interprets it,
that trusts it, and
that is led by it.
The old scroll is a gift that keeps on giving,
as long as there are faithful people
on the receiving end.

T IS FOR TOTALISM

What I know of "totalism" I have learned from Robert Jay Lifton,

an indefatigable researcher who

probed the evil of the Nazis and the Holocaust,

and concluded that the Nazi claims amounted to a totalism

that was all-encompassing,

that allowed nothing outside its control.

Lifton then went on to study other oppressive and totalizing regimes.

He was able through his extensive research to formulate "eight deadly sins" that recur in every such system:

milieu control,

mystical manipulation,

the demand for purity,

the cult of confession,

the sacred science,

loading the language,

doctrine over person, and

dispensing of existence.[1]

---

[1] *Witness to an Extreme Century: A Memoir* (Free Press, 2011), 67–68, 381.

His categories underscore the ruthlessness and inhumanity that is intrinsic to totalism wherever it occurs.

We have seen over time,

- the *totalism of the church* and its claim to infallible truth;
- the *totalism of scientism* and its reduction of knowledge to measurable certitude, with an ominous tilt toward eugenics;
- and now we face the *absolute claims of capitalism* that allows no breathing room outside its domain, intolerant of dissent or resistance or subversion.

The force of totalism in whatever form it may take
is partly coercive and partly seductive,
so that we are often drawn into its claims much too easily.

I do not find totalism, per se, very interesting. What is indeed interesting is the practice of deconstruction
that aims to dissolve its absolutism, a readiness and a capacity to notice and host exceptions to the rule
that have determined staying power in the face of great pressure.

Here, as I think of them, are five "deconstructive" instances in the Bible that aim to refuse and resist totalism. The reader may think of many others as well.

1. Pharaoh is the great exemplar of totalism in the Bible,
with a claim that is subsequently reiterated by
Sennacherib, Nebuchadnezzar, Cyrus, and eventually the
Caesars in Rome.

In the imagination of Ezekiel, Pharaoh can make a grand claim for himself:

My Nile is my own,
I made it for myself.

He presents himself as the creator God—
it follows that Pharaoh would enslave his workers,
and use them to enhance his wealth and power.
He intended absolute rule on every front.

Most remarkably, an instance of his failure is his inability to control
his oppressed slaves who "groaned and cried out."
He could not silence them;
he could not stop their out-loud ache of enslaved bodies;
he could not prevent their desperate cry of hurt and petition;
nor could he stop the inescapable process
whereby the cry of the slaves reached the ears of the emancipatory God.

The slave cry set in motion the divine resolve for liberty
and with it the undoing of mighty Pharaoh.
Pharaoh is a failed totalizer!

2. YHWH, the emancipatory God, is sorely tempted to totalism, and sometimes performs it.

One such instance of divine totalism is the fierce anger of God

in Jeremiah 4:23–26 where the creator God

can imagine and enact the undoing of creation, step by step.

YHWH will brook no rival and will not be deterred in fierce anger.

Except! Except that verse 27 adds a dissenting note.

This may be a divine afterthought. It may be a late scribal addition.

Either way, it deconstructs the preceding holy bombast:

Yet I will not make a full end!

No full end to Israel or to the world! This is a direct contradiction of the foregoing,

as though God's anger is spent or assuaged or even retracted.

3. Jesus for the most part embodies humbleness and vulnerability

and invites his disciples to be the same.

In this final utterance in Matthew, however,

he utters an immense claim concerning his authority

that would seem to allow nothing beyond his governance:

All authority in heaven and on earth has been given to me (Matthew 28:18).

What a mouthful: All authority in heaven and on earth!

Not even Pharaoh would dare voice such a claim;

what prevents this dominical claim from totalism, I suggest, is that the one who speaks is the same one who has been executed by the empire.

His governance is of a different sort;

it does not participate in the oppression of Pharaoh

nor in the grandeur of Rome.

Thus the summons to his disciples is on the lips of one

whose *foolishness* counters human wisdom,

whose *weakness* outdistances human strength, and

whose *poverty* out-yields human wealth.

His claim, for that reason, is not an assertion of totalism;

it is rather an invitation to be in the world differently,

in the service of the executed risen one who disrupts all imperial categories.

4. In his parable, Jesus constructs a practitioner of totalism (Luke 12:13–21).

He is a prosperous, much-blessed farmer whose crops produce abundantly.

He discovered that he needed more storage area to store his produce, that is, his wealth.

Beyond that he congratulates himself on his great success.

He intends nothing now but luxurious well-being for himself.

His totalism is complete.

Except! Except his sleep is interrupted. He had not anticipated such disruption,

imagining himself to be "fool"-proof. Except that night "But God said."

God is no respecter of his wealth or success.

God calls him by his proper name: "fool."

In ancient Israel a "fool" is one who misunderstands his place in the world, who imagines that he is autonomous, and therefore capable of saying "There is no God."

And so the fool is free to enact great wickedness without accountability.

That, however, is all a major miscalculation. In the night "the fool" must face the reality he spends his daylight denying. *The night of vulnerability* breaks *the celebrations of his day!*

5. In his rendition of *agape* love, Paul lines a world without such love. It may be a world

of mortal and angelic tongues,

of prophetic powers to understand all mysteries and all knowledge,

of faith to remove mountains.

Then Paul offers a disruptive "but":

but does not have love;

but does not have love;

but does not have love;

can only be

a noisy gong,

or nothing,

or gain nothing.

A world without *agape* love is dramatically deconstructed as a world of illusion.

In each of these cases, one can imagine being ultimate and beyond response-ability to anyone.

The Bible knows better and insists otherwise.

It is the reality of the Holy God who undoes and disrupts every imagined absolute.

It turns out that the lived reality of our lives is contingent, penultimate, and vulnerable.

Such an awareness may rescue us from all of our hubristic imagination.

Totalism is always imposed from above;

deconstruction characteristically emerges from below.

It is the business of the church to pay attention to and nurture that which arises from below,

that which is sure to disrupt every imagined totalism.

We may be grateful for the carriers of such deconstruction,
those who refuse collusion;
we may give thanks for them,
celebrate their courage,
and pray for their well-being amid their upstream, disruptive, subversive living.
Amen.

U is for Union

The Prussian Union was formed in 1817
the three-hundredth anniversary of Luther's theses in 1517.
Frederick Wilhelm, King of Prussia,
wearied of the theological quarrels in his domain.
In the eighteenth century,
German Protestantism had devolved into rationalistic quarrels.
Consequently the king formed a new church, the Prussian Union,
that brought together Lutheran and Reformed Churches.
Because of its united character,
the new church refused theological quarrels over petty matters,
and allowed great freedom of conscience in interpretation according to
Lutheran or Reformed conviction.
This generosity of spirit was eventually formulated as
"In essentials unity,
in non-essentials freedom,
in all things charity."

The new church was in agreement that the "essentials"
were the doctrines of the Trinity and the incarnation.
It regarded many other claims as "non-essential,"
and it became a church fellowship that did indeed practice "charity."
For good reason this church fellowship came to be marked as "irenic,"
a refusal to engage in theological disputes of the kind that had beset both Lutherans and Calvinists.
The Prussian Union, in response to the many German immigrants in the United States,
sent pastors to form and lead German congregations.

These pastors were largely trained in "Mission Houses," (that is, not in the university),
notably in Basel and Barmen.
These pastors were readily identified as "union men,"
marked by the irenic spirit of the tradition.
In the United States in 1840 the first organizational effort was made to form the several pastors and congregations
into an identifiable community that was known as
The German Evangelical Society (*Kirchenverein*) of the West;
this was essentially a fellowship rather than an institution.
In 1866 the fellowship took the name of

the Evangelical Synod of the West,
then to become the Evangelical Synod of North America.
In 1934, the Synod united with Reformed Churches in Pennsylvania
To become the Evangelical and Reformed Church,
that subsequently entered into the United Church of Christ in 1957.
I write of this "union" because I am a child of this tradition,
and have been shaped by its claims of simple piety with an irenic sprit.
My father, August, was a "union man" ordained in 1925.
I would have found it odd and ill-fitting if he had ever engaged in theological dispute,
as he had the skills of a caring, empowering pastor.
There were in Germany pastors and congregations that refused to enter the Union sponsored by the King.
These pastors and congregations came to the United States in the form of the Missouri Synod Lutheran Church.
During its long history the "union men" were almost always juxtaposed to Missouri Synod pastors
and congregations with their
hard doctrinal stance and their rigidity that followed.
My gratitude for and appreciation of this tradition of pietism is deep and abiding.

In my growing up years, the practice of the tradition included:

- two years of rigorous confirmation instruction in *The Evangelical Catechism*
  consisting in a mix of Lutheran and Calvinist claims.
- an annual Missional Festival that most often featured
  a missionary on furlough
  through which the congregation would, as best it could,
  raise most of its annual mission budget;
- an annual Synod meeting for the area that would be more reunion than business;
- church folk cooking apple sauce and apple butter in the church yard to take as support
  for our Emmaus Homes,
  two institutional sanctuaries for those who were termed
  "feeble-minded."
- a summer week of Leadership Training School
  that instructed in church art, and public speaking, plus
  being great fun.
- a host of young "union men" pastors in and out of our house,
  to me the smartest, most handsome, and winsome people,
  these pastors being a primary impetus for my "call" to ministry;
- a Sunday School teacher, Mr. Borchers, who cared more for us than for the curriculum.

The entire experience was shot through with an "irenic" spirit.

Only late did I come to see that irenic spirit
is what moved us to deep ecumenical engagement,
as I participated in the work of the World Council of Churches,
the National Council of Churches, and
the ill-fated Consultation on Church Union.
In a climate of culture wars that now besets much of the church
I am grateful to God for an ecclesial inheritance
that aims at joyous fellowship without contests for control.
In a culture deeply divided,
the church can be a force for community that owns our differences,
but that requires some disengagement from the propensity of
the United Church of Christ to be "liberal" without further negotiation.
I may finish with a prayer of thanks
for those old immigrants who trusted the gospel,
for faithful pastors and "union men" who innocently and knowingly practiced the faith through their ministerial arts,
for faithful lay people who, grounded in faith, willingly defied narrow-mindedness;
for faithful teachers who preserved the tradition and regularly gave it fresh expression;
most especially for my father August who was a "union man,"

for my mother Hilda who loved the church with her whole heart, and
for my brother Ed, with whom I was ordained,
who provided effective leadership in the church.
We may pray, further, that this irenic tradition of fidelity
may continue to have its say via pastors, teachers, and lay people,
that we may be, given this legacy, a force for peace-making justice.
The Evangelical Catechism ends with this vow:

> "Lord Jesus, for thee I live, for thee I suffer, for thee I die!
> Lord Jesus, thine will I be in life and in death!
> Grant me, O Lord, eternal salvation!"

We prayed this prayer most innocently;
it nonetheless continues to be the point
for those who love the Lord Jesus in every season of their lives.
Amen.

V is for Victory

In the long-ago days of my seminary education

my theological teacher Elmer Arndt

urged us to pay attention to *Christus Victor* and to read it every year in ministry.

The book, written by Gustav Aulen, a Swedish Lutheran bishop, articulates the three

dominant "theories of atonement":

- "satisfaction" by Anselm that issued in a notion of "blood atonement,"
- "moral influence" by Abelard, and
- "victory over God's enemies" by Luther.

Aulen intended that we should see that Luther, via Aulen, had the right understanding,

that God in Christ had won a mighty victory.

(I recall that later on in the congregation where we both worshipped, Professor Arndt proposed as a new name for the congregation, "Christ the Victor.")

Thus I was educated in and convinced by Arndt's teaching;

I understand the work of Christ to be a victory over God's enemies. I have been astonished to discover how rare is the usage of the word "victory" in the Bible:

In the KJV the few renderings of "victory" tend to be translations of *ys'*,

a word we elsewhere render as "save, rescue, deliver."

Thus "victory" is the defeat of enemies who oppress and deny the freedom provided by God:

Concerning God's victory:

O sing to the Lord a new song,
for has done marvelous things.
His right hand and his holy arm have gotten him the victory (Psalm 98:1).

Concerning human victories wrought by God:

He took his life in his hands when he attacked the Philistine,
and the Lord wrought about a great victory for all Israel
(1 Samuel 19:5; see 2 Samuel 19:2, 23:10–12).

In the New Testament "victory" characteristically renders *nike* (long before it indicated shoes).

The most triumphant usage is in 1 Corinthians 15:54–57:

Death has been swallowed up in *victory*.

Where O death, is your *victory*?
Where O death, is your sting?
The sting of death is sin, and the power of sin is the law.
But thanks be to God who gives us the *victory* through our Lord Jesus Christ.

In the NRSV, "victory" occurs more often,
again mostly translating *ys'* (2 Kings 5:11, 13:17, Psalm 20:5–6).
Most interesting is the affirmation of Proverbs 21:31, also *ys'*:
The horse is made ready for the day of battle,
but the *victory* belongs to the Lord.
Thus the dominant usage portrays God's willing power to engage and defeat enemies.
In the Old Testament, the enemies are Israel's traditional political, military threats.
Thus the oldest victory song is on the lips of Miriam (Exodus 15:21).
Miriam sings exuberantly of the overthrow of Pharaoh;
she portrays the combat of YHWH with Pharaoh
as a mighty bodily contest
in which YHWH has drowned Pharaoh, his troops, and his horses.
In the enthronement hymn,
the imagery is still concrete and bodily,

referring to YHWH's "hand" and "arm" again as though YHWH engaged in direct combat (Psalm 98:1).

In the New Testament the combat and victory are no longer against historical enemies:

For our struggle is not against enemies of blood and flesh, but against the rulers, against the authorities, against the cosmic powers of this present darkness, against the spiritual forces of evil in the heavenly places (Ephesians 6:12).

This roster of enemies concerns spiritual forces of evil:

rulers, authorities, cosmic powers of darkness . . .

This catalog of God's enemies in the New Testament concerns characteristic spiritual forces. We may note, however, that this inventory includes "rulers and authorities," so that it is credible to see that these "spiritual forces" may indeed take human—sociopolitical, economic—force and form.

The great doxology of 1 Corinthians 15:54–57:

three times names "death" as a cosmic force of negation

that seeks to undo God's creation by fostering resignation and despair.

The church's singing is saturated with the imagery of victory over death:

Lives again our glorious King, Alleluia!

Where, O death, is now thy sting? Alleluia!
Once he died our souls to save, Alleluia!
Where's thy victory, boasting grave? Alleluia![1]

The strife is o'er, the battle done;
the victory of life is won;
the song of triumph has begun. Alleluia![2]

Thine be the glory, risen, conquering Son;
endless is the victory thou o'er death has won.[3]

Christ has conquered death and sin, Alleluia!
Take the King of glory in, Alleluia![4]

It was a strange and dreadful strife when life and death contended;
the victory remained with life; the reign of death was ended,
Stripped of power, no more it reigns,
an empty form alone remains,
death's sting is lost forever! Alleluia![5]

The church regularly reaffirms the victory of Christ and the rule of Christ;

---

[1] "Christ the Lord is Risen Today," *The United Methodist Hymnal*, 302.
[2] "The Strife is O'er, the Battle Done," *The United Methodist Hymnal*, 306.
[3] "Thine Be the Glory," *The United Methodist Hymnal*, 308.
[4] "Hail the Day that Sees Him Rise," *The United Methodist Hymnal*, 312.
[5] "Christ Jesus Lay in Death's Strong Bands," *The United Methodist Hymnal*, 319.

we are variously alert to the way in which the power of death
does it work
of undermining our human capacity for hospitality, forgiveness,
and generosity.
The singing of the church makes this combat
contemporary in our lived experience,
and therefore the victory pertains from day to day.

At the same time, we must recognize that the church has
largely lost it nerve for such singing,
as we have very much reduced our congregational singing to
love ballads,
and surely worst of all to "praise hymns" that have no plot,
no dramatic movement, and no celebrative witness.
To be sure, this notion of combat and victory is not the only way
the rule of Christ can be articulated,
and recent feminist theology has boldly offered alternative imagery
in the work of such acute scholars as
Rita Nakashima Brock, Katie Cannon, Elizabeth Johnson, and
Delores Williams;
their work runs well beyond the horizon of Bishop Aulen.
The church lives by its dramatic imagery that permits and requires
endless imaginative reiteration.

The world yielded by the imagery of Christ's victory over death
is a world in which *neighborliness* overcomes fear,
in which *generosity* triumphs over parsimony, and
in which *forgiveness* prevails over vengeance.
We need not live cowering before the negations of death,
but we may trust ourselves to the new rule of Christ;
we can join in the good work of remaking the world savaged by death.
We may in boldness
be steadfast, immovable, always excelling in the work of the Lord because we know that in the Lord your labor is not in vain (1 Corinthians 15:58). Amen.

W is for Winnicott

D. W. Winnicott (1896–1971), a Freudian child psychiatrist,
has been of great importance to me professionally and
personally.
Whereas Freud had taken the processes of self-formation to be
internal negotiation
(*superego, ego, id*),
Winnicott, through his practice
saw that the "maturational processes" are not internal,
but depend upon a *dyadic interaction* with a reliable partner,
in most cases, the mother.
Winnicott, in *The Maturational Processes and the Facilitating Environment:*
Studies in the Theory of Emotional Development (1965)
concluded that from the earliest moments after birth,
a young child needs an adult who can be on the receiving end of
the free expression of the child's needs, wants, and desires.
A mother capable of such response he identified as "good
enough" (that is, not perfect),

who permits the child's genuine experience of omnipotence.

Such an experience permits the formation of a strong sense of self.

When the mother is unable to accept such a role,

she may impose her will on the child.

In such a circumstance, the young child early recognizes that she must conform

to the will and intent of the mother,

even if it means denying one's own true self.

Such a not-good-enough mother would evoke in the child a "false self"

that is alienated from the true self of the child.

Thus authoritarian cultures and families produce readily conforming children

who engage in false behavior in an effort to please and gain favor

from the authoritarian adult or system.

Professionally Winnicott's insight helped me in my research

because I was able to see this connection:

in scripture (especially in Psalms)

the "*omnipotence of the child*" takes the form of *lament and complaint*

wherein the speaker is free to speak honestly to God,

and God is reduced to a receptive, responsible partner.

In the most aggressive of such psalms, Psalm 44,

the speaker assumes a tone of omnipotence toward God:

> Yet you have rejected us and abased us,
>   and have not gone out with our armies.
> You made us turn back from our foe,
>   and our enemies have gotten spoil.
> You have made us like sheep for slaughter,
>   and have scattered us among the nations.
> You have sold your people for trifle,
>   demanding no high price for them,
> You have made us the taunt of our neighbors,
>   the derision and scorn of those around us.
> You have made us a byword among the nations,
>   a laughingstock among the peoples. (Psalm 44:9–14)

The rhetoric of the psalm pounds away on the failures of God.
As far as we know,
  God is listening on the receiving end of this barrage.
The psalmist eagerly assumes dominance
  and holds God responsible for all that has happened,
  that has led in turn to shame, disgrace, and brokenness.
When the barrage of hostility has been fully expressed,
  the psalmist is free to circle back with petition;
  it is this God just attacked who is the only source of hope:

rescue,
awake,
rise up,
redeem.

It is like that with a child:
the mother toward whom the child may rage in self-will
is the same mother from whom the child receives required resources for life.
The assertion of such omnipotence permits the relationship
to be genuinely dialogical,
with each party having a turn at primacy.
But alas, the church has largely silenced lament and complaint,
disregarding a lot of the psalms,
and messaging a submissive piety before an almighty God.
As a result, the church all too much is an assembly of false selves under the rule of a top-down God.
Such a top-down arrangement allows no space for honest dialogical engagement.
The psalms of lament and complaint model for us freedom and honesty before the mystery of God.
Personally, Winnicott has been important for me:
My growing up context was not coercive or heavy handed;

but it was distinctly top down
and I was a docile participant in that arrangement.
The top-down pressure was not at all overt, but it was in the woodwork.
That social arraignment readily fostered clarity in relationship,
of youth before elders,
of women before men, and centrally
of people of color before white people.
Only much later, through the hard work of therapy, did I come to see
and understand the force of such forms of social control.
It has remained for me to claim and appreciate the honesty
and freedom that belong to a dialogic interaction with God in which I (and we) can sometimes be the dominant voice.
This discernment of social reality and the hard work required
did not leave me bitter or resentful as it might have.
Rather it led me to an appreciation of an immigrant community
that the best it knew,
that continued to lean upon the wonder of God's emancipatory grace.
The insight of Winnicott increasingly led me,
professionally and personally, to an awareness
of the deep unending struggle in our society

for the practice of a genuine dialogical engagement
between those in power and those who live in response to such power.
The church has most often colluded with the powers that be in top-down certitude;
the capitalist economic system has been top-down,
(which you know if you have ever tried to get a bank loan);
the media has largely become a huckster for selling goods for the capitalist system.
In such a context of top-down authority,
the church has a distinct and very different role to play.
In a *monolithic culture*, the church has a chance to be militantly *dialogical*;
But it can do so only if and when it recovers
the honest practice of lament and complaint
that must not be reduced to confessions of failure.
This in turn will require the church
to delineate the God of the gospel in terms of God's own character.
While the common assumption of "American Christianity"
is God as *omnipotent*, *omnipresent*, and *omniscient*, a claim echoed by authoritarian leaders
with phony offers of certitude,
the God of the gospel, by contrast, is marked

in relational covenantal ways
by *justice*, *righteousness*, *steadfast love*, *faithfulness*, and *mercy*
(see Hosea 2:19–20).

When we are alert about these characteristic markings of God,
and the rejection of Zeus-like mastery,
we may be on our way to identifing "successful humanness"
that cares less about wealth, power, and control,
and cares more for fidelity and abiding attentiveness in every season.

Winnicott invites us the claim of
a "good enough mother,"
who is receptive and responsive to our healthy self-assertion.

Winnicott, further, went on to see
that a "good enough mother" in time, must curb the omnipotence of the child and call to responsible attentiveness.

So it is in Job:
after Job has had his vigorous say of self-assertion (Job 29–31),
God, hidden in the whirlwind, responds in majesty and power
that reduced Job
to "dust and ashes."
Both voices are essential to honest faith,
the voice of Job's self-declaration and
God's self-praise of divine wonder and beauty.

Winnicott understood all of this as he patiently and alertly observed the children entrusted to him.

We may finish with a prayer for all those to whom children are entrusted:

parents, teachers, doctors, pastors,

praying that they will have the wisdom to listen,

the grace to be addressed honestly,

and the courage to speak a demanding word in response.

Such engagement is proposed by Winnicott;

It is modeled in the prayers of Israel;

it is a daily task among us. Thanks be to God! Amen.

X is for Xenophobia

God of all peoples,
  we give thanks that we are your chosen people,
    we Jews, or
    we Americans, or
    we white people.
  We are glad to be special in your sight;
  we rely on your special gifts;
    your special protection, and
    your special attentiveness to us.
We are, alas, surrounded by strangers who are unlike us,
  Palestinians who claim "our" land of promise;
  torrents of immigrants who crowd in on us, or
  people of color who surge around the earth.
We do indeed have fear (*phobia*) of strangers (*xenos*);
  these strangers threaten our way of life: they
    expose our privilege,
    use up our tax dollars,
    take our good jobs,

overwhelm our schools with their children,
bring violence in their wake, and
disturb our accustomed order.
We fear them and wish they were gone.
And then You!
You notice and welcome strangers:
• you saw the scattered Hebrews in Egypt and formed *Israel* from them;
• you mobilized an array of immigrants
—debtors, criminals, land-seekers, fortune-hunters—
and formed *the United States*.
• you watched the many races of people since the Tower of Babylon,
and you formed *white people* above all;
You overcame the strangeness
• of old Hebrews,
• of masses of European immigrants, and
• of nondescript white people, and made us your chosen.
But you did not stop there:
you have continued to notice and welcome strangers;
on the lips of Moses you provided food and clothing for strangers (Deuteronomy10:18);
on the lips of Jesus you saw strangers and welcomed them (Matthew 25:35);

in the memory of Paul you embraced the "unclean" and
welcomed gentiles.

You are the God who sides with strangers,
and provides a home for them;
you act against our chosenness and scatter our specialness all around your creation.

And then, eventually,
you commanded that we, in our time and place, should love the stranger;
you intended that the chosen and the stranger should live according to the same law;
you willed that we should use our energy and our resources for the prosperity of the stranger;
you declared that we, as your chosen people,
should provide care, sustenance, and dignity for those unlike us.

We wish it were otherwise;
We have expected otherwise from you;
We much prefer otherwise.

But we have seen your insistent, relentless passion for the stranger.
We resolve, in your presence, to be a community of welcome,
practitioners of a just generosity for the other,
partners with the other in making all things new.

You welcome saints from every tribe and language and people and nation (Revelation 5:9).
You welcome a multitude from every nation, from all tribes and peoples and languages (Revelation 7:9).
You have authority over every tribe, and people, and tongue and nation (Revelation 13:7).
You proclaim the gospel to every nation and tribe and language and people (Revelation 14:6).

Overcome our fear, enliven our generosity, empower our courage,
that we may be your chosen people alongside strangers who stand with us before you.

You are indeed God of nations and peoples;
that takes some "getting used to," given our chosenness,
but we are resolved to live in the world as you will it.

All praise to you, Lord of all nations and peoples! Amen.

Y IS FOR YHWH

We praise you, YHWH!
What else can we do?
We cannot utter your hidden name;
your vowels do not match your consonants;
we dare, in our stammering, call you "Lord,"
because we do not know a better name for you.
We can only, with a hint of the first syllable of your name, say
Hallelu*jah*, hallelu*jah*, hallelu*jah*!
For all your hiddenness, we cherish what you have shown of yourself to us:
We know you in and through the stories of your action,
with your stunning inventory of active verbs;
above all you are the God who heard the slave cries and delivered them.
You are the God who works transformations:

The Lord kills and brings to life;
he brings down to Sheol; and raises up.
The Lord makes poor and makes rich;

> he brings low, he also exalts.
> He raises up the poor from the dust;
> he lifts the needy from the ash heap,
> to make them sit with princes
> and inherit a seat of honor. (1 Samuel 2:6–8)

You are the God who restores:

> Bless the Lord, O my soul . . .
> who forgives all your iniquity,
> who heals all your diseases,
> who redeems your life from the Pit,
> who crowns you with steadfast love and mercy,
> who satisfies you with good as long as you live
> so that your youth is renewed like the eagle's.
> The Lord works vindication and justice for all who are oppressed. (Psalm 103:2–6)

You are the God who makes provision for all your creatures:

> You open your hand,
> satisfying the desire of every living thing. (Psalm 145:16)

We live in awe of your transformative work that you
exalt the humble and
humble the exalted.

It is no wonder that we love to tell your story!
We know you in your steady recurring work of fidelity:

you are a God merciful and gracious,
slow to anger,
and abounding in steadfast love and faithfulness,
keeping steadfast love for the thousandth generation,
Forgiving iniquity, transgression and sin. (Exodus 34:6–7)

Sometimes it is only "justice and righteousness,"
as you will good to the ordering of the neighborhood;
sometimes it is only "faithfulness and steadfast love,"
as you show generosity toward the vulnerable,
always and everywhere it is your "mercy/compassion"
that bleeds out your goodness toward your creation.
We are grateful for the endless ways in which you
show yourself to be the source of newness for all our
creatureliness.
We are grateful for your many ways of self-giving,
not least in Jesus of Nazareth through whom you show
yourself in creaturely form.
As we enter into your majestic presence,
we are moved to seek forgiveness for our violations of your
faithfulness;
forgive us,

when we distort you in your faithful freedom,
when we script you in our creeds to box you in,
when we seek in our liturgy to manage your authority,
when we have in our morality reduced you to our triviality,
when we have sought in our piety to make you too easily available,
when we have tried in our ideology to cage you in our notions of race, class, gender, nation.
Forgive us for all our efforts to have you on our own terms,
to minimize our majesty,
to limit your fidelity, or
to evade your graciousness.
Because we know better than that,
we resolve to reissue our *calculation* as *doxology*,
that takes you seriously as we know you to be.
We will, as we are able,
love you with our whole heart,
love our neighbors as we love ourselves,
do the urgent work of justice for the oppressed,
do the neighborly work of mercy,
and will do the creaturely work of caring for your creation.

You are the God of our future:
  we do not doubt that you will a just, peaceful creation;
  our hope is in you and in no other, in you alone;
  for good reason we commit to hope,
      to bring our energy and our wisdom and our passion to
      your good purpose,
  that we may do the continuing work
    as a sign of our solidarity with your good purpose.
We join the whole church—on earth and in heaven—
  in glad praise to you,
    giving thanks for your blessing that outflanks our need,
      giving our needs and our hearts to you in trust,
      fully devoted to obedience
        that is our proper posture before your holiness. Amen.

Z is for Zechariah

The priest Zechariah appears in only one dramatic sequence in one of the gospels (Luke 1:5–25, 2:39–80).

His narrative appearance is in two parts:

In the first part (Luke 1:5–25)

he is a priest in the temple;

his wife, Elizabeth, is barren;

he receives an angelic visitation that leaves him terrified;

The angel announces that his barren wife, Elizabeth,

will have a son—John—

who will be filled with Holy Spirit

summoning Israel to repentance.

Zechariah doubts the angel . . . given the old age of him and his wife;

he is consequently struck dumb.

The angelic announcement opens the future in a way not unfamiliar to us,

a child to a barren woman,

a reiteration of the birth of Isaac that caused mother Sarah to laugh,

yet another "impossibility" to be wrought by God.

In the second part of the narrative of Zechariah (Luke 2:29–80),

the child is born;

his name is John as the angel had specified.

Upon Zechariah's utterance of the name indicated by the angel,

his muteness is broken;

he can speak! He voices praise to God for this impossible possibility;

with his restored speech, Zechariah offers his grateful celebrative poetry.

He anticipates the birth of a son to Mary, of the House of David.

He awaits the birth of Jesus,

who will be a mighty savior,

who will show mercy,

who will save,

who will forward the old promise of father Abraham,

who will emancipate Israel for a new offer of holiness and righteousness.

He portrays the coming birth of Jesus as a whole new beginning for Israel,

freed from oppression,
able to live fully according to the holy covenant.
But then the old priest addresses his own son named by the angel,
John:
You, child!
You a prophet,
you to prepare the way,
you to offer life via forgiveness.
John will be a marker for the "tender mercy" of God,
light in the darkness,
a guide toward peace and well-being.
This brief poem of Zechariah contains all the life-giving drama of
the prophet:
from barrenness to birth,
from muteness to speech,
from old world to new world.
The son is strong in the spirit,
waiting in the wilderness,
for the right moment of enunciation.
Old Zechariah joins the company of those in the Gospel of Luke
who sing the new beginning:
Mary in her Magnificat sings of a radical reversal of
economics;
the angels sing "peace" over the birthing village of Bethlehem;

Simeon, a righteous and devout man,
sings a Benedictus for his privilege of seeing God's salvation in the baby Jesus.
John himself will break into song by reiterating the poetry of exilic Isaiah:
Prepare,
Make straight,
See the salvation of God, the same salvation of God that Simeon affirms.
This singing welcomes and articulates a new world,
via John and Jesus,
that can only be sung;
it cannot be sketched in detail;
it cannot be offered as a program or blueprint;
it cannot be rendered with planned specificity;
it can only be sung in a subversive mood that violates the rulers of this age.
Zechariah in his utterance manages to
respond to both surprising babies,
to John the forerunner,
to Jesus the Savior.
And we are heirs of this lyrical affirmation:

we cling to this poetry that defies the closed world of power;
we celebrate the coming governance of holiness and righteousness;
we receive the forerunner with a response of repentance;
The angel cites the final verses of the prophet Malachi,
the final verses of our ordering of the Old Testament;
John will be Elijah reiterated:
the remembered Elijah—so Malachi—
will turn the hearts of the parents to their children
and the hearts of the children to their parents (Malachi 4:6);
the new Elijah will rephrase:
. . . to turn the hearts of the parents to their children,
and the disobedient to the wisdom of the righteous,
to make ready a people prepared for the Lord.
The old alienations overcome;
The old affronts abolished;
The old antagonisms reserved;
no wonder Zechariah could sing in gladness;
no wonder we cherish and reiterate his poetry in our worship;
no wonder we live in hope for the world John announced;
no wonder we receive our life afresh according to this new governance.
Zechariah must be last in the alphabet,

because his poetry is what we have awaited for a long time.
Now it is on his lips,
    and in our liturgy.
        ready for new recital, over and over, in glad receptive
        hope. Amen.